LORD, HELP ME!

Lord, Help me!

LEARNING HOW TO GET THROUGH LIFE

WITH A LITTLE HELP FROM JESUS

By Charity Dockery

Charleston, SC
www.PalmettoPublishing.com

Lord, Help Me!
Copyright © 2020 by Charity Dockery

Hardcover ISBN: 978-1-64990-043-2
Paperback ISBN: 978-1-64990-243-6
eBook ISBN: 978-1-64990-242-9

TABLE OF CONTENTS

INTRODUCTION

Well, here is my moment. This is the time I am supposed to make you think this book is perfect for you
and that you should buy it immediately. This is my
attempt to convince you that this book is more intrigu-
ing than that bestselling book that everyone is talking
about. I apologize. I am not the best at writing a killer
introduction; I realize that. However, I think you will
learn something from this even if it's just a small piece
of information. There is only so much I can say to persuade you to continue to keep reading, but I can tell
you that God put this book on my heart to share with
the world. I have gone through plenty of triumphs and
tribulations in just a short time of my life, and I feel
that my mistakes and decisions have put me in the
amazing place that I am in now.

God has shown me so much through the years
and, more recently, tested my strength in the past

few months. Between life experiences and the Bible, I have grown one thousand percent more in my faith and hope that you can do the same. The stories in the Bible have shown me what normal humans they were and how we still compare to a book that sends us back thousands of years. It has made me feel so much better about myself after learning how people who knew Jesus and watched His work still doubted Him; not that it's good to doubt Him, but we are human, and that's how our brains work, unfortunately. We want answers; we want to see the thoughts and actions played out, and we do not want to have patience for Him to do those things. We are going to experience doubt, pain, frustration, anxiety, and hurt. It is up to us how we apply that to God's word and allow that to transform our minds into what God wants for us. I have had a lot of different things through life that have challenged me and my faith to its very core. I have felt so belittled and so unworthy that I have had nowhere to go but to God. I have had days I did not feel like a Christian, doubted God, and just didn't want to pray anymore. I have had things happen to me I did not understand and still do not understand to this day. God's grace and mercy have brought me through all of it. But it took me seeking Him to find what I have been missing. We all have our own stories to tell, and some do, and others keep them to their selves. I am not saying either is right or wrong, but I think you should consider the things God has gotten you through and how that can really change someone else's life; they might need the push you can give them. I have chosen to share some of my stories in hopes that they will change something in you and show you just how easy it is to let go of your situations and let God intervene. You will never feel completely whole until you surround yourself with Jesus and God's word. Your decisions matter. Your choices matter. What you choose to do today and ten years from now all matter and will make an impact on your life.

So, what will you do? Will you continue to go through this life suffering with pain and anger? Will you continue to be hardheaded and think you know everything? Do you remain skeptical of what God can do in your life? Or will you let God take over and give you the peace you deserve? After years of fighting and confusion, I came to the point that God took over for me, and He gave me the greatest joy and happiness I could ever experience. God will always give the opportunity for you to share these same experiences, but ultimately, will wait for your pursuit. I think we forget that His hand is extended to us every day and night. He is our father and wants to be there for us; He wants to know how our days went; He wants to know what we are feeling, if someone hurt us, and how we need His help. So many of us think that, since He is God, He should already know that information. I hear you, but don't you think our parents know when we are upset, know when we need a hug, and make us feel better after explaining and talking it through? God is the same way. He needs us to be vulnerable with Him and share our bad days so He can help us through it and give us the hug we need. Once I chose to completely let go of being stubborn—thinking that I knew everything and that my plans for myself were better—I was given a sense of peace and was more willing to give all my worries to Him. That day, I finally sat down on my bed in a dark room, sobbing, and said, "Lord, help me!"

I pray that you will be able to increase your faith with God after reading this book. I hope you are able to dive into this book and refer to the Bible for the answers you have been searching for. I pray that you let God's word wash over you and allow new opportunities for you. You deserve peace, love, and hope to get you through your day; only God can give you these things. I pray that you ask God to show you how to be more of a disciple of Christ and how to teach others about His great work in your life. I pray that you can be an influence on others and show them how to be open about Jesus and not allow it to feel like a foreign conversation.

I challenge you in the days to come to have a friend or two that you can open up to about Jesus and with whom you can study His word, even if it's just a random text about something you read in the Bible that intrigued you.

"For where two or three have gather in My name, there I am with them" (Matthew 18:20 [NIV]).

He is right there, guys; He just needs us to gather and allow Him to come into our homes and restore our broken sin.

You can do all things through Christ who strengthens you (Philippians 4:13 [NIV]).

Go forth and move mountains, my friends.

CHAPTER ONE

The Beginning

I remember sitting in my bathroom with my aunt next to me, waiting. I could hear the clock ticking in my head. Not that there was a physical clock in the bathroom, but I could hear each second go by. I felt that minutes took hours; then, finally those two blue lines popped up. The test said to wait five minutes for results. Yet, after just a few moments, it was already positive. I immediately started crying. My aunt stared at the test, making sure it was actually accurate and not just accidently showing two lines. All I could think was, *This can't be true! Is it broken?* She started asking common questions: "Did you not use protection?" "Did you think it was not going to happen?" "Your mom is waiting out there for an answer…"

The whole time, I was crying and texting my boyfriend to let him know that the pregnancy test was positive. He was as accepting as a sixteen-year-old boy could be when finding out he was going to be a dad. We were both unsure what to do. How were we going to take care of a kid? We were too young to live together, and we had to finish school. I was so confused, because this shouldn't have happened to me. (I was aware of many girls having sex, yet none of them were pregnant.) Why did I have to be different? Maybe they were responsible and used protection? Or maybe they just got lucky. All I knew was that I was not the lucky one. I did not get to hide my virginity anymore; I did not get to keep that mystery with a growing belly. I was about to grow up really fast, and I had no clue what was about to happen.

That was the start of Christmas break of my sophomore year in high school. I was on the varsity cheerleading squad and thought I was the coolest kid out there. I mean, I was dating a football player, and we were just living the typical high school life. Basically, everyone in high school was having sex, so why not join the club? I knew of a few girls that had gotten pregnant—older girls that had gotten themselves into tough situations—but I knew I would never let that happen to me, right? I mean, that never happened to all the other classmates having sex with their boyfriends.

Before my knowledge of that day, before that test, all the signs came and went. I started having moments when I was exhausted before we even got to the football game to cheer. My breasts were very tender, and where was my period? I was going to start birth control in like a week, so it was ok if my period was irregular then. The pills would fix that right? I called my mom and asked her for some multivitamins because I was tired and probably just needed some vitamins for a boost. She immediately said, "That's a red flag," and she called my aunt. I'm sure they talked about it all and decided that my crazy self was pregnant and that I had been hiding that I was sexually active. My aunt called and said she was coming to give me a pregnancy test because my mom thought I was pregnant.

My sister and her boyfriend were at the house with me, and they started asking me all the questions that you would hear on the show *16 and Pregnant*. The ones that seem staged because people don't actually ask those questions. It's actually exactly how those moments go for people. They were asking, "What are you going to do if you are actually pregnant?" "Did you not use protection?" "Are you going to keep cheering?" "You're going to have to go through school with a kid?" "Are you going to graduate and finish school?" "You think people will freak out?" "What is dad going to do?" It literally was like a scene out of that show. I should have signed up; I could have made a killer appearance.

We were sitting outside talking and waiting for my aunt to show up. I started getting nervous because— let's be honest—I might've actually been pregnant. What the heck was I going to do?

At that time my mom showed up, I thought, *What the heck, woman? You're supposed to be at work while Aunt Julie comes.* Then my aunt followed behind her. I was told to go pee on this test and find out the truth. Once it was positive, my aunt called my uncle, and he got another test, because how could that have been true if I wasn't sexually active, right? So once one family member came, they brought more for support. My uncle and cousin showed up, and of course, that test turned positive right away. I started telling my mom I had been having cramping, pelvic pain, and spotting, and I didn't know if that was normal. I thought it was my long-lost period coming the past few days. Being a base in cheerleading and throwing girls up in the air and catching them was not the safest thing for my growing uterus. She called around to different doctor's offices, but no one could get me in because it was getting close to 5:00 p.m., and no one can see a newly pregnant teenager that quick. My mom got in touch with an office that was willing to wait after hours to examine me and confirm pregnancy. Looking back at it now, it clearly was God. I have worked in clinics, and there is no way we would have stayed open after hours for a brand-new patient that needed to confirm pregnancy. It requires a lot of work and overtime. I am so grateful that God used that clinic to show my family support and love during our very hard time.

My mom called my dad's job and told them to tell my dad to come home and refused to give them a reason. I will never forget this day. The whole thing was emotionally tragic. My dad walked into the door and stood there with his face so serious and confused. He was leaning up against the front door with one arm supporting him and the other on his hip. I felt like he was looking into my soul, demanding answers. My mom turned to me and said, "Well, are you going to tell him?" I thought, *Umm…Ma'am, are you really expecting me to tell my dad, "Oh hey, I have been having sex with my boyfriend behind your back, and now you're going to be a grandpa…Yay!"? Nope.*

She quickly jumped in and said, "She's pregnant. We're leaving now for the doctor because she's having bleeding and something could be wrong. Here is the positive test. Now get in the car!"

I know what you're thinking; this is some crazy stuff and probably would have made a good drama show. No, this is my life. The whole drive to the doctor's appointment, my dad was just yelling and asking, "When? Where? How long has this been happening? What were you thinking?" I thought he was going to explode. I mean, he basically did, without the smoke and fire. The next hour at the doctor's office was too tragic for me to process at the time. My dad walked in fuming; you could see it all over his face and his body language. The doctor came in the waiting room and immediately told him he needed to wait in there and he was not allowed to go back with me and my mom.

Let me paint you a picture of this: My dad was in work clothes that were filthy, and he had the box with the positive pregnancy test in his shirt pocket. This big, bald/tattooed guy was sitting in the waiting room, ready to attack. Luckily, the clinic was closed, and we were the only ones there. That would have been even more embarrassing—if there was a waiting room full of hopeful older pregnant mothers.

We went back, and they did a pelvic exam and a transvaginal ultrasound. The doctor was very sweet, and he told me that there was a baby about seven weeks or so in my uterus; the baby had a heartbeat and was growing. He told me I needed to be on bedrest the rest of Christmas break and not do anything at all but lay on the couch. My boyfriend was waiting on the other end of the phone for me to text him the news. The car ride home was quiet and extremely tense. I told my boyfriend he was going to meet us at the house so we could all discuss this and prepare for the baby on the way. We all talked like grown adults, despite the fact I was fifteen years old at the time.

That night, the full morning sickness hit (in hindsight, it was probably just nerves), and I was extremely nauseous and ready to puke at any moment. My dad and I had a talk; he came in my room and asked what my plan was. "What do you mean?" I said. He asked, "Are you going to keep the baby?" It had never even crossed my mind that I could have an abortion or give it up for adoption. I told him I was going to absolutely keep the baby and just continue to move on with life. It was time to put on my mom pants and prepare to be a parent.

Where is my faith in all this, you ask? I grew up going to church every Sunday and then some with my family. We attended regularly, and I felt like I grew up in that church. I thought I knew who God was, what sins were, how I should act, and the proper way to respect my elders. I also knew that I was not supposed to have sex before marriage, but school and peer pressure made that hard to follow. When you're young, you do not realize the seriousness and the repercussions of your actions. Acting untouchable and saying that your future self can worry about that is probably the dumbest thing and also totally what I did at the time. My grandmother is a very faithful Christian woman, and I was terrified for her to find out. I knew that having sex before marriage was a sin, and I knew that it would be disappointing to her to know I committed a sin and was now having to live with the consequences. And how was my grandpa going to process this? His little granddaughter was going to be a mother? When I went to my grandparents for the first time after they found out, they didn't say much. They just smiled and hugged me. It was relief to know that I was still being accepted, even after what I had done.

I continued to go to church when my parents went (I was too young to drive myself, so that was my only option). I continued to pray and ask God to help me through the process. It was not easy praying to God knowing that I'd messed up and thinking He was probably disappointed in my actions. Can you think of a time or day that you did something and you knew immediately it was wrong? You felt shame, and you were scared to confront God about your actions? I have had so many times and continue to. We are humans, and it is our nature to sin (thanks, Adam and Eve); that's why we need God to guide us. The good thing about Him is that He knows all. He knew we were going to mess up and sin, and He loves us anyway. He sent His son to die for us because we, being sinful humans, would not be able to be saved alone, with all the terrible decisions we make on a daily basis. It is hard to accept His grace because He is so willing to give it out to those who ask. We expect to get responses from Him that our neighbors give us, usually not very good responses. We get judged, called names; people turn away from us; we get disowned by our close family members; etc. My life would be completely different if I hadn't gone to God and faced my sins and repented. God's grace is something that cannot be taken away from us, and the beauty of it is astounding. You need to experience this.

You're going to think multiple different times that my story is a hot mess, but the best thing is that, no matter how crazy our lives are and no matter what we do, all of our stories matter and are important. Jesus still loved me, even when I decided to make a decision to cause a complete change in how I thought my life "should" have gone. God knows what we are going to do with our lives, but He gives us the freedom to make that journey on our feet. What journeys have you chosen in your life? What decisions have you made that could have potentially changed the course of your life? Where does your faith stand?

Let's look at this from another prospective. What do you do if your child or a young girl says she is pregnant? The first thing we all want to jump to is anger; that's ok. But after the anger, after we realize the situation, the best thing to do for her is to show her love from Christ. The last thing I needed (that I mostly received) was judgment and hate from people in the community. Grown-ups that I should have been able to look up to put me down daily and shunned me like I had a huge giant *A* on my shirt. Don't be that person. We are all children of God, and pregnancy is not bad. Sex out of wedlock is bad, but the sin is done, and we have to be willing to show love and point that person in the right direction to Jesus. We need to support one another no matter our sins. We need to be there to guide the young when they don't know how to do it on their own. Pointing people to Jesus is what we are on this earth to do. Go be disciples of Christ instead of judgmental sinners.

CHAPTER TWO

Coparenting

My sophomore year went by quickly. My daily routine consisted of the following: wake up, throw up, get ready, be judged all day at school, go home, do homework. My parents had to continue to buy me bigger clothes, and I had to adjust my desks in class to fit my pregnant belly. Shockingly enough, high school furniture is accommodating to your average pregnant teenager. I finished out that year with just a few months left until delivery; I was put back on bedrest. My summer was TV, food, sleep, and more food. I had my specific scheduled shows that I made sure to watch so I wouldn't miss anything new.

Once I had Zoey I was able to take off the first five weeks of school. The school allowed a teacher from another school to bring me my homework and help me with what I needed. I spent those days breastfeeding Zoey while working on homework. Starting my junior year was really nerve racking because I was jumping back in and only getting an average of two to four hours of sleep a night. I went to school multiple times with either pee or spit-up on me. I had to balance my homework, being a mom and trying to coparent even though her dad didn't live with me.

My parents were still strict after I had the baby and only allowed him there for certain times, and he had to leave at curfew. I knew we were young, but it was hard to have help from him when we had the barriers of still being teenagers and living under different roofs. My parents were very supportive and helpful as they helped me raise her and made sure I planned to finish school. But let's be honest; raising a child while you're a child is not easy. This was just the start of the challenges I was going to face through my teenage years and into my twenties. What was so hard was the people around me acting like pregnancy was such a bad thing. They liked to remind me every day that I should be ashamed and feel bad about my life. As If the pressure of being a student, teenager, and mother were not hard enough, I had the degrading words from the unknowing mouths of my schoolmates pushing me down. Lord, help me!

After Zoey started to get a little older, things started to change, and my daughter's dad's and my relationship shifted to something that was not healthy anymore. There was a lot of frustration, confusion, and hate that started to grow. We had no clue how to balance life living in separate houses with a newborn. I felt like I was raising her and it was all on me; he seemed upset that he didn't have the opportunity to be able to care for her like he wanted to and knew he was capable of. This was my first real relationship; I did not know how to be a proper parent and partner to my significant other. I was young and only knew how relationships worked from the older people in my life. Not all of them were great for me to look up to, but I was going with what I had to work with. Think of yourself at my age. Did you know enough about functioning in a proper relationship to raise a child? If so, awesome! Teach that to your kids so they have the skills, in case they go through that or their children do. If not, then you're like most of us who didn't know how to process it and just hoped we wouldn't be the next pregnant one.

Have you ever thought about the person(s) you were intimate with and wondered if they would be a good parent to your children? See, people say don't have sex before marriage because it's a sin and against the Bible. Or you shouldn't have sex because you could catch STIs. You know what people don't talk about? Raising a child with someone and having to coparent with that person for the rest of your life. You will have to agree on raising the child and discuss discipline, religion, haircuts, clothes, Christmas gifts, and whether they will believe in Santa. Who plays the tooth fairy? Who pays for sports? How will weekends work? Who gets what holiday?

After a few years, our relationship remained toxic; we were attempting to coparent and hate each other at the same time. I started thinking that my daughter only needed me and I could handle being a single mom like a boss. I was angry, irritated, and I felt like I was the only one putting in the work. If God wanted me to have full custody, you better believe I was going to work to make sure she was safe, taken care of, and growing up with the best life I could provide. God ended up showing me that was not the plan, and I needed to accept that.

We were in court so many times for custody during the first three years of her life. That's some of the hardest stuff to go through because you pay all this money for attorneys and court fees, you argue why your right, you come up with evidence, and you basically battle your case to the judge of why you believe you deserve full custody or what you think needs to happen for the child. It is nasty and sometimes unnecessary. Our last big court date, we went back and forth with our attorneys to prove why we deserved to have full custody and why the other parent didn't. The court decided we needed to have coparenting classes. It was obvious that we hated each other at the time and had no clue how to coparent together. We couldn't see that our parenting style was only hurting Zoey in the end. We then were instructed that we would have to do classes weekly for a certain amount of time. That meant I was going to be late to college every scheduled day and potentially be kicked out of my class for not being punctual and not staying up with the work. I was not going to have time to retake my class if I wanted to get into nursing school. Microbiology was a very important class for my career. My teacher was kind and willing to allow me to come to my class late, and she stayed after class to help me catch up on the lesson for the day and to answer any questions I might have had. Looking back, I was very blessed with that opportunity. I would love to say I came out that semester with an A; no, I C'd my way through that semester. But you know what? I did it, and I am proud of that.

When we started counseling sessions, we sat on opposite sides of the couch and mean-mugged each other most of the time. The counselor told me something during our visits that completely crushed me. She said, "Zoey acts very shy and timid to go to her dad when you are dropping her off; once you leave, she is super excited with him and ready to play. You are influencing her emotions toward her dad because she knows you hate him. You need to change that, or she will always feel that way because of you." Talk about making me feel like a terrible mother. Dang. I thought I was protecting her, but I was only thinking of myself and not how she felt.

The counselor ended with us writing each other letters to basically forgive and let go of the past and start focusing on parenting for Zoey. After I was able to write my letter and let go, God completely helped me forgive him and not let any of the past affect me and my parenting with him.

Whether you are parenting by yourself or coparenting, remember to raise those babies up to know and praise God. Jesus says that children are a blessing from God and a fruit of the womb (Psalms 127:3 [NIV]). If you're fifteen and pregnant, forty and pregnant, or on your fourth kid that was not planned, you should always love your children and know they are a blessing and will change your life, even when you don't think it is the right time or you're not ready. I wouldn't have it any other way with my children; they have blessed me and shown me so many things to help me mature in my life. They bring so much joy and kindness. Whether you have the messiest house or the messiest relationship with their other parent, that child looks to you to have it together and comfort them. You can do it; you can hold your head high and fight whichever way is necessary, because when you have God on your side, anything is possible.

Of course, God's intentions were to have children raised by a mother and father who both love the Lord and can teach their children about Him. That clearly doesn't always happen in this day and age. If you know someone that's a single parent, remind her that God is still with her to support and help her through life. He is the father we all want and is there to father the fatherless. Ephesians 6:4 says, "Fathers, do not provoke your children to anger, but bring them up in the discipline and instruction of the Lord" [NIV]. Whether it's just us raising our kids or its multiple helpful family members, none of that will matter if we are not teaching them the way of Jesus and how to be followers of Christ.

Raising children is not easy. It's very hard work, and they like to press our buttons. God gave you your children to allow you to keep them safe and show them Jesus. But let's not forget that these beautiful children are not ours; they are God's children. We will go through hardship, and some of us will go through worse things than the others. We will not have all the answers for why bad things happen or why we have to watch our kids go through something, but you should have faith in the Lord and know that it's His child more than ours and He has the best plans for the kids. He knows what will happen, and He gives the most comforting angels to guard our kids and protect them. As parents, we have a hard time letting go; let me be the first to say that I am protective of my kids and want to spend every moment with them. But I have to put God above them and know that they are His children that He will keep safe.

I have to do my job of praying for them and showing them His love. Children are so pure, and we could learn things from them every day. We expect to be their teachers, but maybe we should let them teach us sometimes. If I was having a hard day or another stressful day with my daughter's dad, sometimes Zoey would remind me she loved him and was happy to get to see him. She would show me that she had unconditional love for both of her parents, even though we didn't have it for each other. Children exemplify God all the time, and we are just so wrapped up in this world that we forget that. No matter your age, parenting style, single status, or married status, these children need you. I feel so honored that God chose me to raise my kids, and I hope that one day, I will get to see the love of Christ shine through them onto others as they get older.

Remember, we make the decisions that ultimately end in us having children, whether we are married or not. We need to pray for each other, show support, help when it's needed, and parent with our significant others to the best of our abilities. We are not better than each other; we are all sinners, and no one is above us, only God.

CHAPTER THREE

Love

*"You have heard that it was said, 'Love your
neighbor and hate your enemy.' But I tell
you, love your enemies and pray for those who
persecute you" (Matthew 5:43–44 [NIV]).*

I think this is one of the hardest scriptures for us to
swallow. Loving our neighbors includes loving everyone that might have done wrong to us in our lives. That
can include anyone in this world that we might not like
or agree with. It's not easy to sit there and think about
how Jesus walked this earth and still stood by God's
word and loved His neighbors. He was dying on the
cross and still asked God to forgive the terrible people
that were right there killing Him. He said, "Father, forgive them, for they do not know what they are doing"

(Luke 23:34 [NIV]). Talk about how much love and mercy Jesus gave to so many people during His time on earth! I wish I could just have some of that type of love. Well, it's a good thing that I have learned a lot from God and that He has shown me how to start loving like Christ and teach that love to others around me.

Let me tell you a little bit more about some of my days in high school while raising my daughter. Remember, kids in high school are mean, and they love to start drama. I learned quickly that the kids in school were mean, but those parents can be just as judgmental and rude. During my senior year, I was determined to not give up on cheerleading, and I was going to try-out again. After my daughter was born, I was unable to try-out until my last year left in high school. I had my amazing family to support me and watch my daughter while I was at school. I practiced every day and went to private lessons to learn and perfect my captain try-out routine. I put a lot of work into it and was very hopeful I could do it. I felt that I had to prove to the town and everyone in it that my child was not a disability and my life was not over just because I was a mom at such a young age.

It wasn't all flowers and rainbows for me like it was for others. Once parents started finding out I was trying out for cheerleading *and* captain, they panicked and started rumors to try to ruin my chances (not surprising, right?). I had people telling me that "so and so" was hoping I wasn't trying out, and if I was, they hoped that I would not try-out for captain because I was not a good role model for the girls. Let's forget the fact that their kids were doing much worse than I was. All the while, I was just over here raising a child; that was all. I was told that people hoped I wouldn't try to go for fair queen because, again, I was not a good role model for the girls. I tried to let those things just slide off, but the reality is that it was hurtful dealing with the fact that adults were saying these things. I mean, kids are mean, but their parents—they should know better. They were grown adults with their own kids to raise, yet they turned their attention to me.

I had to just keep telling myself that God would deal with them, that it was not my place to judge as they were, and to just forgive and move on (ten years later, I am still working on that). Even now in my life, I have to remind myself that God is the ultimate judge and that is a robe I do not wear. I now have learned that I must show love to these people, even when my flesh wants to be angry and not forgive. I mean, they probably have no idea how bad their words hurt at the time, but since I do, I have to learn to forgive and love them just like I love God.

I tried out for cheerleading and captain. Here is where I tell you I made it and proved myself to all of those people. Wrong! God had different plans for me. I did not make it. I was devastated at first. I cried and was confused about how I was supposed to show how I was a badass and prove these parents wrong. I was worried that the judges did not grade correctly because of some of the other girls that made it while I didn't. But then I realized that God wanted me to focus on graduating with my daughter. He knew I did not need to be away from her cheering at games and practices with people that did not respect me as a student or mother. I also realized that I needed to be a parent and stop trying to prove myself to people who did not deserve it. I needed to raise her to be the best girl she could be. Cheerleading was very fun, and I do miss it some days, but that's all it is: cheerleading. It's not something that showed me how to care for my child, how to deal with the criticism of the town, or give me any important life skills. It was fun while it lasted, but it was not going to ruin my life if I was not a cheerleader my senior year. When I look back, I think of how miserable I would have been and how the town would have talked more about how I wasn't a good role model. God definitely protected me in that stage of my life and allowed me to focus on my child and loving her. I also wouldn't be with my husband now if I had made the team.

It ended up being a rough year between my daughter's dad and me. We broke up right before I started my senior year. We were trying to raise a baby while not living in the same house. We both had school, and he was attempting to start a new job in the real world after high school. Our relationship was toxic, and we caused more headaches and negative attitudes toward each other than we caused anything positive.

The good thing about love is that it doesn't always have to be hard. It doesn't always have to be you focusing on trying to love the hard people. Sometimes, people walk into your life, and it's like a breath of fresh air. Their love is so genuine, and it spreads like wildflowers. That's the love that's my favorite and I want more of. God shows us that love through relationships, marriages, kids, and family. I found that love quickly with my husband.

Tyler and I started dating a little bit into my last year of high school. He knew my past because he went to the same school as me and we had been friends since middle school. We were really good friends in middle school and the start of high school, but we eventually fell off and just didn't talk much. I, of course, due to life-changing situations, was now a mother and not involved with much besides my daughter. Tyler and I started talking more and more and ended up going on dates. He was a little awkward, of course, knowing there was a child involved, but he dived in immediately and was ready to conquer those changes and do life with me. He was there for me during all the following troubled years with me and my daughter's dad. Through the police being involved, attorneys, custody battles, and my emotional momma tears. I could not process how a seventeen-year-old boy was willing to be with someone that couldn't just drop everything and go on dates. He chose to come over and hang out with me and my daughter on a Friday night watching *Barbie* instead of going to the football game.

I didn't understand why he still stuck around. He was questioned plenty of times by others and myself about why he would choose me instead of someone that he could have a "normal" dating life with. He received a lot of judgment from others, and I asked him multiple times if he wanted to run and told him I wouldn't be upset. His sweet self would just sit there and tell me that he was there for me and not going to leave me because of my situation. God blessed me so much by allowing me to have such a great man to help me raise my daughter. I really didn't understand at the time how he could stay with me and show me so much love, when most people in my community were doing the opposite. We graduated high school together, and I was so happy to show everyone that I could do it. I could graduate with a two-year-old and had plans for college. Before I got pregnant, I didn't see why college was important. Not many of my family members went to college or even graduated high school. Tyler had some set plans for his college years and what career path he wanted to take. I knew I had to get my crap together and figure out my degree plan and actually go through with going to college because no one else could provide for her like I could.

I always dreamed of becoming a marine biologist. The animals, the ocean, and my whole career focused on caring for ocean life. It just sounded so delightful. Moving away to live on the ocean was what I was most excited about. My daughter and I could get a condo or small house to rent on the ocean, I could work on homework, and she could play in the sand. It was a dream for sure. Then reality hit me. How was I going to raise my child alone three hours away from family? How was I going to get accepted into a college that required almost a 4.0 for you to be considered? What school would I put my child in, and would it be a safe environment? I am not saying I wasn't capable or smart enough, but it was hard to focus on making a 3.5 or higher in high school while changing diapers. I wanted to still try and not give up on my dream, but I felt like Jesus was shaking His head, thinking, "Let's be real Charity. You need family support, and you are not meant to study ocean animals. I have much better plans for you than living near the ocean alone."

Well, he was right. I had more in store for my future and my daughter's future than moving away and attempting to do all this life alone. Also, I was not about to leave Tyler behind and force us to live in different towns that were hours away from each other. God had shown me so much love from my family and friends that I didn't want to leave. I was getting a lot of negative push back from some of the community, but God showed me His love was bigger than them and their opinions. I didn't need to run away from a town just because it was highly opinionated. I decided I wasn't going to attempt to get into a college way out of town and would continue to live with my parents as I got going in my big girl life and applied for college.

Lord, help me! What career was I going to do?

CHAPTER FOUR

Anger

Do you remember those days after graduating high school when you thought about how fun college was going to be and what it would be like to be a "real" adult? I was thinking that as well. With my two-year-old, I was going to go to college and get a full-time job. Tyler and I stayed together after graduation, and we were both going to start at the same junior college together. He had plans to transfer to Texas A&M, but I had no clue yet what I was going to do. I immediately got a job waitressing at a local restaurant a few days after graduating and started taking prerequisite classes. I had no clue what I wanted to major in. Marine biology was out the door. Business was extremely boring to me, and science was cool, but I doubted my ability to major in it. I needed something practical.

I started really thinking about how obsessed I was with learning about the human body and decided that nursing wouldn't be a bad idea. I would almost always be guaranteed a job, no matter where I moved. I knew nursing would have challenges, but, like, I could handle it, right? I decided to start taking all my classes for nursing: science, ethics, psychology, more science, etc. Everything was going pretty well for me: homework, work, raising a child, school, hanging out with Tyler. I was still in the period of not getting along very well with my daughter's dad, but I would think, "No biggy." I know what you're thinking: "Grow up and get along for the sake of your child." I wish it was that easy at that time, but it wasn't. We had real issues and problems to be worked on, stupid issues that needed to be let go. Satan had his way with our relationship for some time. It took going through very impactful and complicated issues for us to mature and be responsible parents.

I would think about things that would upset me, and my list would slowly go on and on. I would think of my anger toward coparenting at the time, my anger toward classmates that were mean to me, my anger with teachers or parents of classmates that would come into the restaurant and judge me for being a waitress; and the list would go on. I tried praying about those things, but the hate and anger was so high, Satan would stomp over my prayers and turn them into more hate. Let me share a huge moment of anger, frustration, confusion, and complete distress that I had to go through. I want you to focus on how you would feel going through this and think about how you could put God in the place of the anger. I know our circumstances are probably different, but those feelings can be the same with all of us.

I remember this day like it was yesterday. My grandmother was watching Zoey for me while I was at work; she told me that Zoey really wanted to stay the night with her. Normally, I would say no because she watched her all day and would do so for me again later in the week. I didn't want to overwhelm her with Zoey's very hyper self. But this day was different. I said yes; it would allow me to get homework done and talk to Tyler all night. The next day after school, I went to pick up Zoey, and my grandmother asked me to take Zoey to my mom so we could talk. We all lived on the same property, so that was a quick drive up the road.

Once I returned, she proceeded to tell me that Zoey was telling her stories about inappropriate encounters she'd had. I knew there had to be a reason she wanted to stay the night with my grandma, but I hadn't thought it was because she wanted to talk to her. I'd assumed she wanted candy all night and cuddles in bed with her momo. My three-year-old was saying things that no three-year-old child should even know how to say. She was saying words that most adults do not even understand. As I left her house and attempted to comprehend what she had just said, my mother told me we needed to talk. "What now?" I asked. She said that Zoey was making accusations to her about the exact same thing my grandmother just told me. Umm…two people, one day, twenty minutes apart hearing the same story from my three-year-old. At different times. How does this happen? Clearly this was not okay, and something needed to be done. I decided to file a police report and let the professionals step in. What else could I do?

I couldn't just sit there and not do anything. The sheriffs came and got statements from all three of us. They informed us that we needed to meet their deputy in the morning so Zoey could talk with someone and possibly have an exam. I couldn't actually process what was happening. Many questions were asked, an exam was attempted, and many counselors were introduced to her. My daughter, who loved princesses and watched *Despicable Me* four times a day, was now saying explicit words that she never should have heard or known until she was an adult. That next day was probably the hardest day of my life. I sat in a hospital room waiting for my little girl, while she was being questioned and potentially examined in the other room.

After a while, they called me into the room with her, and the nurse said that she was not allowing them to examine her, and they asked me more follow-up questions. She seemed totally fine and happy and did not seem to be affected by what was happening. Thankfully, her innocent mind did not understand the severity of the situation. I sat there and saw all the swabs and equipment on the Mayo table that they were going to use to collect samples with. I couldn't process how I'd let this happen. I knew it was out of my control, but as parents, we blame ourselves. We left the hospital to go home, and they told us to keep doing normal daily activities so that she wouldn't suspect anything was wrong or get scared. That meant it was time for more *Despicable Me* and *Barbie* all day.

The following day, we ended up at another place where Zoey got more questions thrown at her by counselors, and I got to sit there in the other room again and wait. They took her to a different room with another counselor, and the police were on the other side recording the conversation in case any valuable evidence was discovered. I asked myself, during most of these days, if what I was doing was right? Was she going to remember this? What if they thought I'd made this up? How was this affecting my daughter? Should I have just left it alone and hoped that she wouldn't remember and that it wouldn't happen again? I was worried that I was putting her through this detrimental experience and that nothing would come out of it. What if she remembered and was then terrified for the rest of her life? I did not want to create difficult memories and cause her to be confused or upset with me. But honestly, what can you do? I chose to stay strong and did everything in my power to protect her and keep her safe.

Investigations typically take a while, and they told me it was hard with toddlers because they had to differentiate between what was true and what was possibly not. Days went on. Zoey continued to tell me things, and I could not comprehend where she'd learned them or seen them. The counselors were still not getting enough answers. I would get some positive news that they'd received new evidence but then some negative news that didn't help our case. I continued to work to pay for my attorney. Most of my shifts consisted of me hiding in the bathroom talking to my attorney or one of the counselors.

"Lord, help me!"

That was all I could say at that point.

I have always considered myself a Christian. I grew up in church, knew God, and prayed a lot. But sometimes we never really know how to pray or talk to God until something crazy happens. At least, that's how it was for me. This was one of my Jesus moments. I prayed for God to help me; help me understand what was happening, show me what I should do as a mother to protect her. I prayed every day for understanding about why she had to go through this, why I had to go through this, and how could we fix this from here. The next few weeks continued with me attending the grand jury, taking her to counseling, and attempting to stay up with my classes and continue to work. Working was hard to focus on, school became harder, and the nights got longer. After working and playing with her, I would have to stay up late and focus on studying for tests and getting my homework turned in on time.

I never got an actual answer as to whether this had actually happened to my daughter. There was not enough evidence. Not enough was located to put anyone away in prison. Since I was a mom, this was the worst news for me at first. I had no way in understanding whether something had happened or why. No closure, no consequences; only complete confusion and frustration. I questioned God so much during this time. I spent most nights crying in my bed, because I'd never pictured my life like this at nineteen years old.

I know what you're thinking: What the hell? I did too. I had to just pray and give the whole situation to God. I knew my being angry and stressing about the situation was not going to help Zoey; it was not going to change what happened or didn't happen. It was just going to eat me alive, consume my piece of mind. It felt impossible to focus on being a mother and getting through school. I wasn't able to enjoy my life with her in that moment, since I was fixated on a situation that I couldn't control.

That situation showed me again just how much I needed Jesus. I needed Him to give me peace about the situation, give me hope that it would be better in the end, and give my daughter what she needed to continue to grow as a little girl, even with this potential "rock" in the path of her childhood. I didn't want her to remember it until she was ready to hear the situation—or maybe she would never even need to know. I never wanted to say something to her to alter her thoughts on what I think. I want her to make those decisions on her own. God helped me a lot that year; He gave me the strength to make it through that situation while also working and going to school. I did not fail out of class, and I was able to mend a relationship that I hadn't known could be fixed. All was well.

Do you still pray and praise God whenever things feel well in your life? I wish I could have said yes at the time, but I didn't really stay strong in my faith after that. I tried to pray occasionally, but being in your early twenties and trying to figure out life is not easy, and staying a Christian was harder when I didn't have a solid support system to follow. It was easy for me at the time to go back to living my life for myself and my daughter. I would focus on my school, dating Tyler, and raising her. I didn't realize I should be talking to God and allowing Him to take the lead in fighting my battles. I always thought I was supposed to be strong and fight it on my own. What I didn't know at the time is that's the beauty of God. We do not have to go to war alone; He has already overcome the world. Why not let Him take on your struggles while you sit and look pretty? That sounds a lot more relaxing than doing it all on our own.

CHAPTER FIVE

Judgment

We are some judgmental people, aren't we? I apologize if you think you are not, but I know I am, and pretty much every human on this world is. We have our own opinions, and we all do things differently. It's our human nature to assume something of another person if that person does things differently than we do. We make the typical confused face or the awkward laugh when people do something that's weird to us, and we can try to think its ok—but deep down, we're totally judging them. The problem is that so many people like to do it, and they like the gossip that goes with judging. They use excuses, like someone brought it to their attention, and they are not hurting anyone if the person never finds out. But it doesn't matter who you talk to or know. God knows everything you do, and He is the ultimate judge that will be there on judgment day to question your every move.

> *"There is only one Lawgiver and Judge, the one who is able to save and destroy. But you—who are you to judge your neighbor?"[Emphasis added]" (James 4:12 [NIV]).*

I just love reading scripture when it makes a statement and it's just like mic drop. I mean, it doesn't get clearer than that. Who are you to judge? What makes you think you're any more capable or better than your neighbor? What makes you think your life is better than the lives of others? How are you spiritually more connected to Jesus than they are? Unless you are Jesus, you're not any better. Jesus is the only human that was just like God and was able to walk this earth before us to show us how to live. I know that I am not anything close to Jesus, but it's a goal I want to live toward daily. Acting like Christ is the most important way we should strive to follow each day.

In my early twenties, I was not walking like Christ at all; I was hardly even walking through life. We hear many stories about how kids are brought up Christian but, once they start getting out on their own, they kind of sway away from that life. I was one of those, once college rolled around. I mean, I knew how to go to God if life got tough. But I didn't understand how I was supposed to pursue Jesus daily. I would try some days and try church some Sundays, but I honestly wasn't trying very hard. I was judged by others so much through all my teen years that I was more focused on getting started in my career to prove myself, and I didn't think focusing on God was my main focal point. I thought getting their approval was more important than God's approval.

After I graduated nursing school, I moved out of my parents' and started my career and adult life with Tyler in a new town where he was attending college. I got a job working in obstetrics and gynecology at a big organization. I was really excited to start my career and expand my knowledge. We had a variety of patients, and I learned something new every day. In my work, I dealt with plenty of pregnant patients, some who wanted to be pregnant and others who didn't want to be. Everyone thought I wasn't old enough to be a nurse because I was a twenty-one years old and looked like a twelve-year-old. I had multiple women say, "It must be nice to get through school so fast and easy." There were comments and assumptions made only from the surface; they didn't know my past. Whenever I informed them that it was not, in fact, "easy" because I was raising a child at the same time, some would apologize. It was always rewarding telling those comment makers that I didn't have it handed to me; I had to work extremely hard to get to where I was. I was used to my hometown, were most older people would question what I was doing with my life or only want to know what was successful in my life. No one would just come up to me and ask how my daughter and I were. It was always, "What are you doing with your life? Are you in school? What's your end goal?"

I will never forget about how I had a patient ask me about my schooling and career, how I went through school, and if it was hard. She then proceeded to say, "Oh I'm sure you had a lot of support and plenty of people to help you through it. Your life must be great." It was super sarcastic, and it upset me tremendously. I was happy about everything I was able to accomplish, and I didn't think having support was a bad thing. I appreciated all the support that I'd had going through school and all the help I'd received financially and emotionally. I shouldn't have had to feel bad for that. I think people that are doing worse off than you feel better about themselves or make excuses for themselves by putting other people down and assuming their lives are prefect and easy. But you know what? We all have our own stories, and we should not write off our own accounts without that knowledge. No book should be judged as just a pamphlet. I am working on not being so quick to judge myself. You and I do not know what Carol on 2nd Street is going through, so we cannot be the ones to judge what she is wearing or how her hair looks.

> *"Therefore, confess your sins to each other and pray for each other so that you may be healed. The prayer of a righteous person is powerful and effective" (James 5:16 [NIV]).*

I feel that we can never be told too many times to stop deciding what we do not know. We should be praying for each other and lifting each other up. We will be judged on judgment day in heaven by God, and we will be expected to answer for our actions.

The Bible says, "Do not Judge, or you too will be judged" (Matthew 7:1 [NIV]).

It's intimidating enough to know God is going to show us everything we have done over our lifetimes when we meet Him. If we can take just one sin away, I think we can agree that judgment is an easy one to drop. This way, we can start seeing people the way Christ sees them.

I had an encounter at work that really tested my strength to resist judging someone. I was still working in OB/GYN at this time. I answered a call, and there was a frantic adult on the other line that had just found out she was pregnant. She was not happy because she did not want to be pregnant because she was in college and had older children in school. She was calling to inquire about a way to have an abortion or where she could go to get it done. I remained professional, but it was very hard. When I was fifteen years old, pregnant, and raising a baby because of my choices, I accepted what God had chosen for me. But you're telling me, a grown adult is not going to raise this baby because it's inconvenient for her? Luckily for me, my job did not partake in that option. So she was sent on her way, and I will never actually know what she decided to do. I could only pray for her and for her next decisions. I was definitely guilty of judging her on the other end of that phone call. But just because people make decisions that are not what we agree with, we still do not have the right to treat people as less than ourselves or judge their circumstances.

There was a time when I received a lot of judgment that I probably didn't even know about. It started when I was legally allowed to drink. We all have those great drinking stories and love to tell about the times we got hammered while in college with all our friends. It's all fun and games when you don't have responsibilities to worry about or children that are watching. I know "it's fun," and "what's one night going to hurt, right?"

At this point, I was a twenty-one-year-old living in a college town. My daughter went to her dad's every other weekend, and I took all that time to party. Some friends lived with us, and others would come up to visit for the weekends. Every weekend that Zoey went to her dad's, I would get drunk. It helped me to avoid thinking about how much I missed her, and it was so fun... at least that's what I thought at the time.

Again, I went down the same rabbit hole of the perfect idealization of life. I didn't go to church and only prayed if something bad was happening or I was stressed about something—selective praying. I loved those weekends when we got to party. We all hung out, watched football, went to bars, and played games. Most of the time, we stayed at our houses to drink because I refused to lose my nursing license from drunk driving. Most of my Sundays were spent sleeping until the afternoon because I'd stayed up drinking really late the night before and usually had a huge hangover. Church was not at the top of my list things to attend on Sundays. I would tell you, all the time, that I thought I was a good Christian and just living the life of a twenty-one-year-old. I thought I would be fine as long as I prayed sometimes and was careful not to do what I considered bad things.

That's the problem with us young adults that we don't even realize at the time. We think we're invincible; one more shot won't hurt; sleeping with one person isn't terrible; smoking isn't terrible if it's only when I drink. The classic "Jesus turned water to wine; He knew how to party." Wrong. Jesus was at a very class party, and His mother helped make Him into the man that He became by showing the power that He had from God. Jesus wasn't in a bar with people dancing on the table; He wasn't just like, "Yo, we're out of wine. I gotch you." He was being present with friends and family at a party, and His mother told Him it was His time to show others His capabilities. He knew once He did that, He was starting on the road that would end in His crucifixion.

After about a year or two of constant parties, I started feeling guilty, and I couldn't keep ignoring it. I started realizing what I was doing was not something that was appropriate, and it definitely wouldn't be a story in the Bible. I wanted to change, but I didn't have the manpower to do it on my own. My husband and I had just bought a house, and we agreed it was time to have a baby. I wanted another child, but it would also be very helpful for me to completely quit drinking. Zoey was six at the time, and I knew she was ready to be a big sister. She had been begging me to have another child since she was three years old. Don't get me wrong. I was going to miss those drunken nights and miss sleeping half the day. But something in me knew that it was not a good lifestyle and that it was not something I needed to continue. Let's be honest. It wasn't "something" that was telling me this wasn't what I needed to do with my life; it was God dropping hints that I needed to refocus and be an adult and a full functioning mother. Zoey was not with me during those nights of drinking. But what was I going to do if something happened to her, and she ended up in the ER? How was my intoxicated self going to get there and comprehend that there was an emergency going on with her? At the time, it was a distraction to ease her absence, but a mother never takes a day off.

Multiple different college students will tell you how fun it is to get dressed up and go out with your friends or have a house party and all just hang out, get wasted, and play games. I am not saying it's the worst thing to do, but how "great" would you feel constantly getting hammered on a Saturday night at the club then going to church on Sunday and praising God for all He has blessed you with this past week? It's almost a slap in the face, I feel. Yes, Noah did get passed out drunk in the Bible. But, no matter your age, addiction to alcohol is not a game, and getting help is the best thing people can do for themselves. People who are going through those challenges need a friend there and not someone who is going to judge them on their actions. Sometimes, we don't just need clinical help; asking the Lord for help can go a long way in your faith. The book of Proverbs says that, if someone is drinking to get drunk or even tipsy, it's not wise. The Bible also says that it's prohibited. Remember, through your faith journey and study of the Bible, you will learn a lot of different ways that we as humans sin every day. That's just how we are made; it goes back to Adam and Eve. But that does not give us an excuse to continue to sin each day because we know "that's how we are genetically geared." We have to make a conscious decision every day to walk and live as Christ did, not as we want to. God gave us Jesus to show us how we should live. He knew people wouldn't listen if they only knew of God in heaven. He gave us a human version of Himself so we could follow the ways of Christ and learn how to properly live our life for Jesus.

"Gracious words are a honeycomb,
sweet to the soul and healing to the
bones" (Proverbs 16:24 [NIV]).

We should treat one another with kind and loving words, instead of mean and judgmental words from Satan. As much as someone might anger you and make you think saying hurtful words will make you feel better and feel superior of that person, it won't. It will literally make you feel like crap afterward and will accomplish nothing in the end.

Remember, "Who are you to judge your neighbor?"

CHAPTER SIX

Anxiety

If you had to think of someone you know right now who suffers from anxiety, how many people would you think of? Does it include you? We all have some sort of anxiety in our lives and can agree it's not easy to over-come. Multiple people that I know, including myself, have suffered from anxiety at some point in their lives. Some more than others, but it continues to cause issues in our daily activities. You can and will defeat anxiety; you can get your life back without the worry day in and day out. You can get to a point where you don't need medication. How you ask?

How do we get to a place where there is more peace than worry in our minds? We live in such a terrible world right now that we worry whether our kids will be ok at school, whether we will get to have a normal day at work without something bad happening. We worry that the world will shut down again over another new disease and cause a panic. I have multiple daily thoughts of things that make me anxious. I have thought about counting how many times I think of worrisome things, but honestly, it is exhausting just thinking about it.

What I have learned is that the only way to get full peace and relief from anxiety is through Christ Jesus. We can take medication as an aid to get us through some tough times, and it will calm us and balance the hormones in our brains. I am a supporter of medication to get you through your hard time and provide you some relief so you can regain your focus. The only problem is that you will always feel there is an empty hole in your heart if you do not have Jesus in your life to help you through those tough times. He is the ultimate healer and the only thing that can truly help you through your storm. Medication can help to an extent, but medication does not trump God; He can move mountains.

I had multiple hard seasons in my life; I had to get on medication to help me through some of them. It definitely helped calm me down and allowed me to focus on things other than crying over my situation. The problem was I was still missing a vital part. I started pursuing Jesus with everything I had; it didn't happen overnight, but I got to a point of complete peace with God, and I was able to get off the medication, still have a happy life, and function like a human again. I was at peace knowing He was capable of fighting my battle; He could do things I couldn't even dream of. I was able to get to a point where I was happier off the medication, because the joy that God gives us is so much bigger than this earth. The joy you can get is overwhelmingly beautiful and calming. I want you to be able to be at that place in your life. I want you to be accepting of whatever God decides to throw at you and to have peace knowing His grace and mercy is worth more than your anxious thoughts.

> *"Do not be anxious about anything, but in everything situation, by prayer and petition, with thanksgiving, present your requests to God" (Philippians 4:6 [NIV]).*

Did you catch the end? "Let your requests be made known to God." The verse does not say that God knows everything; therefore, you do not have to pray and ask for His help. Everyone loves to throw in, "If He is God, then He should know what I am thinking, and I shouldn't have to beg Him for help." That's like saying, "My husband can read my mind, and I expect him

to know I want the laundry done before I get off work."
Now, how dumb does that sound? He may know you
want that laundry done, but if you don't communicate
it, you cannot expect the outcome you're hoping for.
The same goes for God; He may know you want help
and need His help through your storms. But He needs
you to ask for it. Communicate with Him and tell Him
your worries. That scripture says you need to let God
know what you want done, let Him know your expec-
tations, and let Him know you're believing in Him and
His plan for your life.

> *"Cast all your anxiety on him because he*
> *cares for you" (1 Peter 5:7 [NIV]).*

God cares for you more than your parents do, more
than your family does, and more than your spouse
does. He made you exactly the way you are because
you are a perfect child of His. He knew what challenges you would face, and He has equipped you with
what you need to get through life. Your life is just
as important as the life of the celebrity you see on
TV, as the life of the preacher at your church, as the
life of the person that you think has it all together.
All God wants is a relationship with you and for you
to be able to trust, with your whole heart, that He

will take away all your pain and fears. He is just a prayer away if you ask Him to take away your anxious thoughts. Remember to take your thoughts captive and give them over to God; He is able to handle those thoughts much better than you can.

I think part of our problem is that we try to do things on our own so much as humans, and these are things that God has already taken care of for us. Satan loves to remind us that we are lonely, sad, little people that cannot handle what life throws at us. He wants you to think that you are unworthy and do not deserve love from God because "He is too busy for your petty requests." Please, do not allow Satan to make you think you are alone in this world and will forever live with anxiety. You are worth more than that, and you deserve to be free and have peace over your life. God will literally talk to you about any small thing that is bothering you, but you have to open up first.

The translation of the Bible I am using—NASB— has a really cool chapter in it. In Matthew chapter 6, it literally has the title "The Cure for Anxiety" as it starts verse 25. Verse 25-34 is Jesus discussing why we should not be anxious. He claims that the birds don't worry about the things we worry about, and yet they still get to eat because God feeds them. They get to fly wherever they want and go to new locations, and they do not have to worry about food because God always provides. He gives a few more examples, but I think His strongest statement is "You of little faith!" He knows we have little faith, and it is astounding to Him that we cannot trust Him. It's more astounding to me that He still loves us and shows us mercy when we question Him every single day. Guys, this was written like 2,000 years ago, and we still have not learned. This is why the Bible was provided for us—so we could learn from Him, the creator of the whole dang world.

God knew we needed to be reminded over and over of His greatness. I want to highlight the last two verses from this chapter.

Verse 33 says, "But seek first His kingdom and His righteousness, and all these things will be added to you."

He is not telling us to figure out our lives, He is not saying we need to find all the answers to make it to heaven, and He is not saying we need to be prepared to take on all life's obstacles by ourselves. He literally says to FIRST seek His kingdom and His righteousness, and THEN all these things will be added to you. Do you realize that's all He is asking of us? He just wants us to seek Him, and He will literally give us all that is needed to have a life worth living. We make things so much more complicated than they need to be, and

Jesus literally gives us the answers we keep asking ourselves. The Bible is full of answers to questions that I guarantee you are asking yourself all the time. We have the answers; we just decide that our interpretations and our decisions are better.

Verse 34 says, "So do not worry about tomorrow; for tomorrow will care for itself. Each day has enough trouble of its own."

God knows that each day is challenging for us as Christians because we live in a world full of sin. He knows that every day we will need to remind ourselves how to be children of God and watch our words and actions. He knows that we cannot mentally handle the stress of worrying about every day while trying to live through our current days. We are not God; He is the only one that can handle the stress of thinking and knowing what each day will bring. Stop worrying that you need to be Him and take on that responsibility. You were not put on this earth to try to take over His job. He created you, and He will decide when you will go out. You do not need to know the details in between; rather, you need to be more focused on seeking His kingdom and finding the ways to make sure you get there one day once this life ends.

There are multiple things we can think about and stress about all day, but the reality is that these worries are just keeping us preoccupied with things out of our control. I can sit here and spend about an hour thinking of all the things I need to do and plan for the next day and the rest of the week. I will sit here and make a calendar and planner, and I expect everything to go just as smooth as expected. I will then start panicking because something was canceled or because my daughter just decided to tell me a project is due tomorrow and its already 9:00 p.m. I start becoming anxious about my job tomorrow. What if something happens that is beyond my control? Then next thing you know, I'm thinking about what will happen in five years—will I be where I want to be in my career? And then I'll remember that my kids are getting older—and what if they stop loving me?

Now, how stressful was it to read that? I'm pretty sure you can relate to some extent. Don't you want to just tell me to chill out and take a deep breath? That's what Jesus wants you to do. Sit down, take a deep breath, and ask for His help. We need to just switch our focus to Jesus and learn more about Him. Seeking Him and finding out how to be sure we will get to meet Him one day. That's my ultimate goal. Is that not yours?

CHAPTER SEVEN

Marriage

Over the years, God has really started showing me what His intentions are for marriage and how He created it to be. Marriage is supposed to show the relationship between Christ and us—we are bound together with unconditional love for each other. It's a little ironic, because we are all sinful humans and tend to turn our backs on Christ throughout our lives—but He is always there for us. What this shows us is that husbands and wives go through some hard times and it's up to us how much we are willing to fight to come back together. All of our marriages either have gone through or will go through trying times. That's a fact, because we live in a world with sin.

No one has a perfect marriage, even if they try to convince themselves otherwise. God originally started out with Adam and Eve as the first couple. Most people know the story, but I want to point out that they were the first marriage and they were completely vulnerable with each other. They could walk around naked and spend their days in the garden with no worries. They could completely focus on each other and on tending to the garden with God. They didn't have social media ruining their relationship; they didn't have family giving negative input. There was not another person trying to ruin their relationship. They had nothing to compare their love to besides God. Their love for each other must have been so open and amazing. I think we all envy that just a tiny bit. (We will ignore the fact that they committed the first sin and doomed us all…I'm kidding…but really.)

> *"This is why a man leaves his father and his mother, and is united to his wife, and they become one flesh. Adam and his wife were both naked, and they felt no shame" (Genesis 2:24–25 [NIV]).*

We all know marriage is not easy. We have to be completely selfless if we want to have a happy marriage. Marriage is about being one together, not about you becoming the marriage and letting the other tag along.

Once you are married, you are putting your spouse's needs before your own. You should strive to make them happy, compliment them, seek God with them, put your spouse above the kids, show them love and mercy, and forgive them even over the silliest things. Your spouse is your partner; you made a convent when you got married to love each other through the crappiest things in life. We are all human and have a sinful nature, so we will mess up at times. But that's why God's there, along with His word, to guide us through it.

> *"Marriage should be honored by all,*
> *and the marriage bed kept pure; for God*
> *will judge the adulterer and all sexually*
> *immoral" (Hebrews 13:4 [NIV]).*

Marriage is so important to God that scripture says it's to be held in honor among ALL. That means it's not to be held lightly, not something you just decide to do for fun with a random person. You need to be serious and on the same page with your spouse before tying the knot.

Marriage is not something that, once you get bored, you quit. You fight for your marriage because you chose to spend the rest of your life with someone once you said your vows. I have learned that a lot of people (including myself at times) have our priorities completely off. This does not apply to everyone, but most people need to have their priorities together to be able to live their lives the way God intended. That being said, the first thing at the top should always be Christ. Christ is above your kids and spouse. How do you expect to be able to love your spouse and kids if you do not know how to love Christ as He loves us? You will not be complete in a marriage or as a person if you do not fill your cup with the unconditional love of Jesus. You will always be searching for something to fill your void, when in reality, you're missing Jesus, who alone can fill it. I would catch myself putting plenty of other things in front of Christ and letting myself get sucked into the world more than Jesus. Talk about feeling lost when He is replaced with the sin of the world in your head.

Second, your spouse comes before your children. Did you catch that? Your small child that needs you twenty-four, seven does not come before your spouse. Obviously, the children need to be tended to, but once they are comfortable and helped, your spouse should be your priority. It's harsh, but you choose that marriage usually before having that child. It's very easy to want to be with your kids at night or take your kids with you on a date because "it's just dinner anyway." No. Even if you are gone all day from your kids but your spouse wants date night, your children will eventually respect the decision and want to have a marriage like that when they are older. They need to see us working for our marriages daily. You cannot expect to have a lifelong marriage without nurturing it every day. The grass is always greener when you take care of it and water it. Don't just skip to another yard because you didn't tend to the original one. I feel that people forget that their spouses' needs come before their own. We are very selfish people and usually only think of ourselves. But your spouse's needs should be your focus before yourself. You should want to make them happy, make them feel loved, show them mercy even when you don't think they deserve it, forgive when you want to be angry, and just do those dang dishes for them even if you hate it the whole time. Making them feel special will make them want to make you feel the same way. Remember to say thank you to each other, even over the smallest things. Learn their love language so you know how to show them love the way they want to receive it, not how you think they should.

Be aware that marriage is a big deal to God, which means the devil will want to destroy it. Always be on your toes and ready for what Satan will throw at you. He will test your faith and try everything he can to ruin your marriage. He will try to take your spouse away, to manipulate you to do wrong, or to just make you both think you're not compatible. Don't give him the opportunity to ruin something so beautiful.

You can do all things through Christ who strengthens you (Philippians 4:13). Forgive as Christ forgave you, love as Christ loves you, and show grace even when it's not deserved. We can all be followers of Christ; it's time to show it in our marriages.

The next big thing in marriage that can be completely hard is forgiving your spouse when they have done wrong. Forgiveness is the same whether it's a friend, a family member, your kids, your spouse, or even a stranger. God looks at us all equally as His children. He does not choose which one of us is the worthiest of forgiveness. Remember that when thinking of the people you need to forgive in your life.

Matthew 22:39 (NIV) says, "You shall love your neighbor as yourself." Jesus gave His life for us all to be free. This includes murderers, fornicators, adulterers, liars, etc. We are not better than one another, and we are not better than the people that hurt us. Let's talk a little about forgiveness in general. A wise person once told me that forgiveness means you completely move past the situation that has upset you so your feelings are now joy and peace from God. We are responsible to forgive others and accept apologies from them even if apologies are not given.

That does not mean we have to forget the pain we went through. To forgive means to love them as Christ loves us, and it means to completely be at peace with them and the situation. I was also reminded that "love holds no wrongs and covers a multitude of sins" (1 Peter 4:8 [NIV]). Once I forgive someone, I am completely giving that person a clean slate, and I am no longer able to bring up the past regarding the things I have forgiven.

> *"Be kind and compassionate to one another,*
> *forgiving each other just as in Christ God*
> *forgave you" (Ephesians 4:32 [NIV]).*

The enemy is going to put tidbits in your head every time you try to pray for forgiveness. He is going to play them in your head like a movie and remind you why you hated them in the first place. You immediately have to pray and say, *"I am taking those thoughts captive and will no longer allow them to be a part of my day."* After you say that each time over and over, the thoughts will stop. I promise they will. It took me consciously saying this in my head over and over, like a broken record, every day, usually more than once a day. Honestly, what are those thoughts helping with? Literally nothing. They are just reminding you about the negatives, and no fruit is coming from that to help you grow in your faith. It's the enemy's trick to persuade you that you cannot get over what others have done. He wants you to dwell in that situation for years and years if he can keep you. Do not allow him to do that to you.

Now, when we're talking about forgiveness in marriage, it's a whole new ball game. You have your lovely spouse that you made a covenant with, and there really isn't a way to break that. No matter how mad or bored you are together. One thing I hear a lot, when people start talking about being bored with their significant other, is how they don't know if they picked the right person. People like to use that as an excuse to justify their decision. The reality is that, once you decide to marry that person, they are now considered the right one for you. You have to put in the work to make it the right marriage. Make it the marriage you expect and act as you want your spouse to act toward you.

Divorce is sadly a really common thing in the world right now. How many times do you learn on TV, on social media, or in a magazine about another celebrity that was divorced? Or how many times in a small town do you hear about so and so having issues in their marriage and filing for divorce? What does the Bible say about it? Scripture says the following:

> *Some Pharisees came to Him to test Him. They asked, "Is it lawful for a man to divorce his wife for any and every reason?" "Haven't you read," he replied, "that at the beginning the Creator 'made them male and female,' and said, 'For this reason a man will leave his father and mother and be united to his wife, and the two will become one flesh?' So they are no longer two, but one flesh. Therefore what God has joined together, let no one separate." "Why then," they asked, "did Moses command that a man give his wife a certificate of divorce and send her away?" Jesus replied, "Moses permitted you to divorce your wives because your hearts were hard. But it was not this way from the beginning. I tell you that anyone who divorces his wife, except for sexual immorality, and marries another woman commits adultery." (Matthew 19:3–9 [NIV])*

If you catch the end, it says the only exception is sexual immorality. Divorcing because you disagree or decide you no longer like each other is considered adultery. Its harsh and not an easy pill to swallow. But I do want to point out that just because sexual unfaithfulness might have happened in a marriage does not mean that both parties have to give up and divorce. God hates divorce, and He can restore anything you allow Him to be involved in. The book of Hosea in the Old Testament is about a man named Hosea who is married to a prostitute. It talks about how he forgave and did what God asked. The main summary of the book is that God uses Hosea's relationship to demonstrate how He feels about the Israelites' actions and sins. God tells Hosea to marry a promiscuous woman and have children with her. He says that, like an adulterous wife, the land is guilty of being unfaithful to Him (Hosea 1:2). She then turns back to her ways; she sleeps around and gets sold into slavery, and Hosea is without a wife. Now, any normal human would have been like, "Bye, Felicia. You made that decision and got caught." I would not have wanted to go through the heartache of buying my spouse with my money, bringing them home, and then trying to forgive them. That sounds painful. But God went to Hosea and said, "Go, show your love to your wife again, though she is loved by another man and is an adulteress. Love her as the Lord loves the Israelites, though they turn to other gods and love the sacred raisin cakes" (Hosea 3:1 [NIV]).

God is showing that His love knows no wrongs and, even if the people turn on Him and worship false gods, that He has so much love, He is willing to forgive and help them. Can you imagine being Hosea and having to show that much love and forgiveness? If Hosea can do that, can't we? We should be willing to show forgiveness as Christ shows it for us. We should be willing to fight until the end for our spouse that we have become one with, no matter the pain and years of healing we have coming. If we truly love our spouse, then we can look at it from a different point of view. God has already forgiven them; now it's our turn. Don't get me wrong. I know it's not that easy, and some spouses are not willing to put in the work, but you can still do your part and forgive them. If your marriage story ends in a divorce, then put in the work to forgive and to start putting your focus on God instead of the negative things.

> *"Then Peter came to Jesus and asked, 'Lord, how many times shall I forgive my brother or sister who sins against me? Up to seven times?' Jesus answered, 'I tell you, not seven times, but seventy-seven times'" (Matthew 18:21 [NIV]).*

I love this scripture, because it reminds us that, even if we forgive someone and they sin against us again, we should be willing to forgive them again. There isn't any second or third stick when it comes to Jesus. Just remember that we sin every day and God forgives us each and every time.

Marriage is supposed to last a lifetime; we will have to forgive all throughout our life in marriage. We have to put our spouse's needs above our own and have a tender heart toward each other. Put in the work and love to keep your marriage afloat. Don't give up because it gets tough or boring; you will have some of the biggest blessing after the worst storms. God turns the bad things into good for His glory. Your story is not over; Jesus can restore anything you allow Him to work on.

CHAPTER EIGHT

Counseling

"Where there is strife, there is pride,
but wisdom is found in those who take
advice" (Proverbs 13:10 [NIV]).

A Christian counselor was THE smartest decision I made recently. She took my brokenness and messy situations and showed me how to turn them into a blessing from God. She completely changed my thinking and showed me how to become more like Christ and taught me how to act like Him. I went through a time in my life that was completely detrimental and made me question God daily. I needed to find someone who could coach me in the right direction and show me the love of Christ, when people were telling me the opposite. She showed me how to take my thoughts captive and start trusting God and seeking Him.

My sessions with her were like talking to God, except in physical form through her. I was able to talk about why I was angry, hurt, upset, and there was no judgment. I could cry and sit in silence, and she would continue to encourage me and show me Biblical evidence to back up what we discussed. I was able to grow closer to God and have a normal conversation about God that didn't feel foreign to me. I have always felt weird talking about God around people or discussing what I think He is doing in my life, because no one does that anymore. I don't have many people around me with whom I can just sit and talk about what God and I have discussed or what I feel like He is saying to me. Counseling allowed me to be able to do that. It allowed me to be able to just feel normal. I liked the fact that she made me think hard about my choices and decisions. I had to think literally WWJD in certain situations. She wouldn't let me brush it under the rug and hope for the best. I'd done that for so long, and now it was time to bring that out and sift through all the crap I'd ignored and see where God was when I thought He'd left.

She showed me how to fight for my marriage and fight for my children. I had to learn exactly how to be a wife and how women are supposed to be respectful and loving to their husbands. I realized the way I was parenting and putting my kids in front of my marriage was going to cause problems. I learned what boundaries mean and how to put my foot down and follow them. Boundaries are very hard, but they can have the most rewarding outcomes when followed. It took my reading scripture and googling what certain verses meant for me to understand how to read the Bible and what God might be telling me. I would google different stories in the Bible to see how some situations ended up or how Jesus helped them. I was able to use websites that were designed just for questions about the Bible, and they were very helpful. I still use them to this day, almost every night, just to read about new things that I didn't know were in the Bible.

When I first started going to sessions, I was in a time when everything stood still and my life felt that it had flipped completely on its head, different from what I'd thought it was going to be. Satan took that and ran with it. He told me that I wasn't good enough, that I wasn't made to have a happy life and family to raise my kids in. He told me I wasn't worth it. I believed what he was telling me. I believed all those hateful things, because that was the only way I could cope with what was happening. How many times has Satan told you those things? How many times has he belittled you and shut down your dreams? This is why I had to see a CHRISTIAN counselor. Because most of the time, when you're going through something hard in life, it is because of a spiritual battle you don't even realize is happening. You can have a regular therapist; there isn't anything wrong with that. But when you have a Christian counselor who has studied the Bible and knows Jesus, you get more out of your sessions than just coping mechanisms. Getting to know God and figuring out my plans with Him was much more rewarding to me.

Back when I was applying for RN school, I felt the urge to actually start seeking God more, not just pray once a week and never go to church. I thought that I was not doing well in the area of Christianity and started to buckle down studying Him as best as I could. But I didn't get into the program I hoped for and was super bummed. One day, I built up the courage to ask God why I didn't get into nursing school, and He said to me completely plain as day, "Why should I allow you to go further your education in nursing when you do not read MY word or further your knowledge of ME." Well, ding dang it. If that doesn't make you realize your priorities are out of whack, I don't know what will. I knew it was time to buckle down and start learning about this God I thought I knew.

I started to go all out; I bought a Bible, started reading it, went to church with my sister, listened to podcasts, and focused on involving my children with God. But, even doing that, I still needed guidance, strength, and understanding that only God could give me. I needed to find someone that could help me through it and show me how to get the answers I was searching for. I knew I needed God to give me those answers. I needed Him to take the pieces of my faith I'd started on and show me how to glue them together. I wanted Him to help establish a strong foundation for me that wouldn't be ripped apart next time something happened to me in my life. I needed to take the start of my Christianity that my family showed me over the years and build it up to something I'd never known was possible for myself.

When I first started going to counseling, I would vent and word vomit about all the things that were hurting me or the people that hurt me. I would go on and on about what they were doing that affected me and never thought to look at myself. She pointed out my ever-pointing finger. "Me?" I asked. "We are not here to discuss me." She started pointing out that my identity was in my past. I only focused on moving forward in life if I was proving myself to others. I wanted to finish school and have these big titles and successes so I could prove to everyone that my fifteen-year-old pregnant self could do anything I set my mind to. What I didn't know was that my identity was in Christ. You are also a child of God, and your identity is in Him. Jesus provided us with our new lives after His death, which means we are no longer slaves to sin. This allows us to have a relationship with God just as Jesus did. God knows the plans for our lives, and if we are walking with Him, then we should be proud of where we are in life.

My therapist called me out and asked, "Are you not proud of how far you have come?" No one has asked me that, so I didn't know how to respond. The Bible tells us that we are children of God and He is our ultimate creator, so He is the only one we should want to prove ourselves to. God created each and every one of us as His own, and He chose us very carefully, He slowly chose which traits He wanted us to have. He did not create us to be judgmental humans; we chose that and continue to do that through generations. He gave us the freedom to choose how we want to live and how we are going to let others' opinions affect us.

I learned that I do not have to prove anything to anyone. I am happy with my place in life right now and don't see my shift in focus from my school to my family and myself as a failure. I am allowing myself a break to figure out my life and focus only on God and His plans for my family and me. We are supposed to be disciples of Christ, and as Christians, we should be out on the streets showing others the amazing gifts of God and how He can help us all through our lives. People watch us, you and me; they watch us to see how we are going to react to situations. They want to see what we will do and how we will act as Christians. It's up to us to show how Christ would react to these situations, and that's by showing unconditional love. People will hurt you over and over, and the best way to react is by praying for them and showing them love. Not everyone is able to do it alone; that's why we have God.

"In their hearts humans plan their course, but the Lord establishes their steps" (Proverbs 16:9 [NIV]).

"Whoever gives heed to instruction prospers, and blessed is the one who trusts in the Lord" (Proverbs 16:20 [NIV]).

Proverbs is such a good and inspiring book in the Bible. I love the two scriptures above regarding the mind and giving attention to the word. We all think we have our own plans, and we think about what we want and do, but the Lord always directs our paths. He chooses the right path for us and waits to see how we will respond. We are supposed to trust in Jesus and trust in His plans for our lives. He gave us His word for us to read and study to learn more about Him. It says, "He who gives attention to the word will find good" (Proverbs 16:20 [NASB]). The Bible is a living word, and every single time you read it, you will learn something new and read something in a different way than you did before. Having a Christian counselor there with you as you're learning the Bible, learning how to work through your emotions, and learning how to respond like Christ can increase your learning and enhance your understanding of Jesus.

If you find yourself in a moment where you think you need help and someone to talk to, go find yourself a counselor and make sure they know Jesus. Having someone that holds you accountable and teaches you about Jesus can be the best decision you ever make. We all are able to do things better when we have someone holding us accountable and giving us homework to do. We cannot go into this world alone; God puts people on this planet for us to be able to bond with and have positive conversations with. Don't hide in your filth alone; we all have filthy lives every now and then, and we should be there for each other for support and love.

CHAPTER NINE

Not Today, Satan!

I realize it's weird that I'm using a whole chapter to talk about Satan. Do not think for a second that this is going to be praise, by any means. I am using a chapter of my book to tell you about his lies and deceitfulness so you do not waste a chapter of your life allowing him to alter your thinking. Satan is out to attack us, and if he can ruin one more life and keep us away from God, we are just another tally. Do not be a mark on his wall where he counts how many souls he has stolen or ruined with his wicked ways. No matter what you think or might be going through, Satan is watching and ready to attack you and your family. You have to be aware and on your guard. Be prepared for him to attack when you just are becoming a Christian, getting closer with God, reading the Bible, or starting to follow

God's plan for your life. He has nothing better to do with his time except do everything he can to ruin our lives. Satan has told me so many lies that I believed, it's embarrassing. Plenty of people will tell you, "Oh, don't think that way!" or "You know that's not true; you're a good person." But their words of encouragement are tremendously quiet when you have Satan whispering in the other ear.

LIE NUMBER ONE

Having sex before marriage is fine since everyone else is doing it. There is a lot of peer pressure in school, and of course, you cannot be the weird one not having sex. It's not bad; it feels good and makes you look cool. I remember thinking that I shouldn't let my parents tell me what I can and can't do in my sex life; it was mine not theirs. How dumb is that? And my hardly fifteen-year-old mind believed it and kept secrets from my parents and got pregnant in the beginning of my sinning. The main thing sex was made for is to conceive children, and out of all the people in high school that didn't get pregnant; I got to be the statistic.

There are so many people who believe that sex is a necessity before marriage because they have to know if they are worth it or whatever other doubt the devil uses to tempt you. How bad would it be if you married someone who is bad in bed? (That was a sarcastic voice, if you couldn't tell there.) Once people start having sex in one relationship, they find it necessary for every relationship following; because you already did it once, right? You've allowed a new level of what sin you accept as normal.

> *The Bible says, "But since sexual immorality is occurring, each man should have sexual relations with his own wife, and each woman with her own husband. The husband should fulfill his marital duty to his wife, and likewise the wife to her husband" (1 Corinthians 7:2 [NIV]).*

It specifically states that we should not be hopping around to random people to have sex with them. It is a sin, and we need to repent. Satan thought he'd won and ruined my life, but God completely turned it around and made it into a beautiful story for me. Just remember that, each time you have sex with a new person, you are allowing a tie between your souls, and you will forever have that guilt or feelings for that partner. You will need to repent and ask God to free you from that. You would be surprised how God can change thoughts of temptation when you allow Him to. It does not matter what your past is like. God can take you back to a place of purity if you allow him to.

LIE NUMBER TWO

My daughter's dad and I will never work out and he is just useless anyway, so I might as well hope he leaves. For the longest time, throughout the tough years, I wished I did not have to worry about sharing Zoey with him or having to put up with the whole situation in general. I thought she would be better off if I just got full custody and raised her myself. False. God requires two people to come together to make a child because the child is meant to have two parents. God knows it's hard to raise a child, and that's why He made two people to raise our children. There are things I cannot give her that she needs from her father, and there are things he cannot give her that she needs from me. There is not one child that is solely meant to have just one parent. I understand that, in some circumstances, this is the only option and is the best situation, depending on the safety for the children. I am just talking strictly about God's intentions when He created the reproductive system. Children need to learn from both parents, so my being petty and thinking only of myself during those times was a lie from Satan as he attempted to have me raise a child without a father. If you find yourself in a similar situation, remember it's about the child's needs and not what our selfish desires want.

Children need to see their parents working together no matter if the parents like each other or not. Be a positive influence on these babies' lives.

LIE NUMBER THREE

Zoey is going to suffer her whole life because she is not growing up in a stable home with BOTH her mom and dad. When my relationship with my daughter's dad did not work out, I had guilt because I was not able to raise her up with me and her father as a couple. Instead, she would have to go back and forth between our homes. I know I didn't want to have him a part of her life at first, but once I accepted that, the guilt kicked in that my daughter would never have the stability of both her parents under the same roof. Mom guilt was strong as I thought about how my daughter would grow up watching her friends having both parents together or her cousins living with both parents. I still think about how it might be affecting her as she is getting older, going back and forth on holidays and birthdays. But, when we made the decision to split up, she was one year old. She has grown up going back and forth, and to her, it's normal. She loves getting to have two Christmases and going on multiple summer vacations between her dad and me. She gets to be loved by both Tyler and me, and we still get to show her a stable home with us. She gets love from her dad's side of the family. She gets to create relationships with his fiancé's family and gets more people that love her.

As I was going through these lies in my head, I had to consider whether I would allow Christ to change me and do what is in God's word. Luckily, my therapist showed me how to change my thinking and not listen to those thoughts in my head. The Bible talks about taking your thoughts captive. It's amazing what can happen if you tell yourself that, every time you get those thoughts.

Every time I got those thoughts, I would tell myself they were not needed and I was going to take those thoughts captive. EVERY SINGLE TIME I thought about any disturbing thoughts regarding my relationship, I would ask God to take those thoughts captive and allow me to think of the positive things and the happy things regarding my life, husband, and children. I did that multiple times every day for weeks, and finally Satan got bored with me because he realized I was not going to allow him back in my life to ruin anything else he'd already tried to take over.

LIE NUMBER FOUR

You are not capable of completing school with a high degree. Once I had my daughter and decided to go to college, I thought I could only do the minimum certificate/degree. I went to LVN school and graduated. I then finished my associates of science degree. I knew I wanted to go to RN school but didn't think I could manage getting my bachelor's or anything farther. I kept thinking my children were a crutch that didn't allow me to go any farther in my career. I finally realized that, if I wanted my end goal to be a master's in nursing and a position as a nurse practitioner, then there was nothing stopping me but my own mind—and Satan changing it. You can set your mind to whatever you think you are capable of. You do not have to settle for less just because Satan has convinced you otherwise. Of course, you need to be praying about your plans and seeking God; just because my mind is set that I can get a masters one day doesn't mean that's what God has planned for me right now. But just know that Satan is the reason you think you're not good enough. You are good and capable; you don't need him in your ear causing destruction. Remember, he loves to remind us we aren't good enough, smart enough, or capable of doing anything remotely hard. I just tell him, "Not today," and I move on with my day. Keep your head up and focus on what you and God have for your life.

We are responsible for our thoughts. We are responsible for continuing to let this devil take away our joy. It is up to us to take those thoughts captive and change our perspectives. Our minds can get us into trouble, and if we allow it to alter our thoughts and remind us of negative situations, we are going to end up miserable and unhappy. Remember to take your thoughts captive from sin and replace them with truth. Replace them with who God says you are and not who Satan thinks you are. God loved us enough to allow His son to die on the cross for our sins. If He was willing to do that so many years ago, He is still willing to love you and be your ultimate provider. You are special, you are wanted, you are a child of God, you are not worthless, and you are who God says you are; you are worthy of His presence, and you are unique. You were delicately crafted by God to accomplish big things in life. Satan is a liar and should no longer be allowed to take over our lives. God put us on this world to share the gospel. Satan will try to stop you and convince you that you are not good enough or smart enough to accomplish the task. You can guarantee that Jesus will equip you with the proper tools to be able to share the word no matter how much Satan might try to stop you. We are stronger than Satan and will always be bigger than him when we have God in our lives.

CHAPTER TEN

Alone

I want you to think about your life; let's say that there is someone you love or trust, and all of a sudden, she is gone. Disappeared. Either she is gone because she chose to leave, or maybe she passed away, and you feel like there is no way to move on. Thinking about life without that person seems impossible to manage. Have you gone through this before? I think we have all experienced some sort of death in our lives or death in a relationship. Maybe some of us have experienced someone completely abandoning us. They left us there alone without explanation, and we have to try to put the pieces back together. Does that sound familiar to you?

I know this topic isn't easy, but I want to share some input and information that I learned while I was reading the Bible. When I start thinking about how to process my grief, it sounds overwhelming and frankly scares me. People think you are supposed to grieve a certain way and act a certain way because that's how they did it. But the truth of the matter is that we all process grief differently, and how we handle that is between us and God. We can process it alone, with supportive friends, or even with a counselor. In the end, when we put our trust in God, we are no longer alone. He is our comfort, and we can only find the overpowering peace through Him.

I just recently finished a Bible study, and it talked about Jesus's life, resurrection, and return. I really started thinking about how some of the people watched Him die on the cross and how detrimental it must have been to watch. Can you imagine having to watch His suffering and watch how brutal they were to not only Jesus but also to the men on the other crosses next to Him. His mother stood alongside Him and watched her son be tortured and treated like dirt. She couldn't do anything to help Him; she could only watch Him die alone on the cross. As a parent, I cannot even process what she was feeling at that moment. As parents, we feel that we are supposed to protect our children; in this case, her child was telling her this had to be done for God. I love God, but having to watch that and feel helpless is enough suffering for anyone. After Jesus passed, I would assume they started to grieve and try to move on with life as best as they could. The Bible does not say much of what the disciples did or what Jesus's mom did after His death, unfortunately. But, fast-forward a little bit, and I find it interesting how people reacted after Jesus ascended back to heaven. Jesus stayed around for forty days to preach about the kingdom of God after He'd risen from the dead. He ascended back into heaven and said that He would return one day, but no date was given. What I picture is all of these people and His disciples that He'd taught for so long just staring into heaven and thinking, "What do we do now?" Looking up and asking, "Are we just supposed to stay in this spot and wait?" He was their teacher and leader. What now? He showed them what to do, how to help people and heal people. He showed them how to properly live their lives, and now He was gone, and there was no word on when He planned to return:

> *After he said this, he was taken up before their very eyes, and a cloud hid him from there sight. They were looking intently up into the sky as he was going, when suddenly two men dressed in white stood beside them. "Men of Galilee," they said, "why do you stand here*

looking into the sky? This same Jesus, who has been taken from you into heaven, will come back in the same way you have seen him go into heaven." (Acts 1:9–11 [NIV])

I know death and abandonment from someone you love dearly is very hard to process. But I want you to think about the emotions these people were feeling. They were able to be in the presence of Jesus for so long, and then they watched Him die, come back to life, and leave again. They were completely on their own now. They were no longer followers; they had to become the leaders. They had to live the rest of their lives not knowing if Jesus was coming or if they would ever see Him again in person. They were not instructed to act like Christ and spread the good news of Jesus, without Jesus. They were taught how to do that alongside Him but didn't realize they were being taught what to continue to do when He was gone.

We go through that off and on with people in our lives, and we have to remember they are no longer present; it's time we start focusing on what God's plans are for us. We will have seasons of hardship and grieving, but we must not stay in that position forever. It's normal to take some time to grieve and try to understand what is happening with our lives. But sooner or later, we have to change from followers to leaders. Maybe we need angels to look down on us and ask why we are just staring up waiting. I know of multiple times I could have used that push.

I went through a season where I thought I was being abandoned, and I was completely beside myself. I didn't know what was happening, I didn't know what I'd done wrong, and I wanted to know how I could change it. But you see, the problem was I kept saying, "I did something. This was My fault. I should have done something better." You catch how I made it about me? I made it about what I did or didn't do. What I didn't realize is that God put me in a position where I had nothing left distracting me from finding Jesus. He was able to switch my focus from everyone else to Him and showed me what He was capable of. I needed Him to remove people from my life, because He knew I couldn't progress in my Christianity with the distractions I had at play. I didn't even realize it until I had nothing else to focus on. It completely made me into the Christian I am today, and I honestly have never been so blessed before.

I tell you this—about how it changed my life—because I want you to know the best is yet to come for you, my friend. Whether you have gone through this in the past, now, or in the future, just know that He will take every bad situation Satan tries to steal and change it for His glory and ours. You can always guarantee there will be more blessings at the end of your storm than you could even imagine; just be patient.

When you feel completely down and unsure of how to go on with life, just remember that Jesus is right here with you waiting for you to ask for help. He will never abandon you. Even if you think He is being silent, He has not gone anywhere. If you are going through a tough time or trying to understand His plan, all you really need is to ask for His peace to get you through it and the joy to help you each day. He has the capability to replace all those emotions with complete peace. You shouldn't ever have to feel alone in this life when you have Jesus in your heart and the Holy Spirit to guide you.

I want you to be at a place where you can walk away from your spot, no longer starting at heaven confused, and be able to go lead people in the direction of God. I want you to be the one questioning others about why they are still standing still and not helping you lead. This life is so temporary compared to eternity; don't waste it on natural things we cannot control. Keep your head up, friend; you're a leader now.

CHAPTER ELEVEN

Prayer and Healing

Once you go through something detrimental, how do you heal? How do you move past something that caused you to feel so broken and empty? You cannot be healed to full completion without God. You can do things to help yourself through it and make it easier to accept God's healing, but you ultimately need Him in the end. You also need to find out where your happy place is so you can think and keep your mind clear. When we have so many people in our ears telling us what we should and shouldn't do, it creates a fog that makes it hard to hear God. You need to give yourself space away from the mess and be silent for a little while.

I always like to go run when I feel upset or stressed out, that's my happy place where I allow myself to think without anyone else's opinion. It allows me to calm my brain with some good music and exercise. There is just something about some Christian music that calms my soul, and running allows me to take my anger out (even if I can't breathe because I am out of shape). This particular day, I had a lot of anger and sadness I needed to take out. I was angry, sad, and hurt that I hadn't gotten an explanation regarding my current situation. I was frustrated that I had no control and just had to sit back and watch.

That day, I chose to run. I went to the high school track in my town; I put on my headphones, tied my shoes tight, and took off running. I ran lap after lap with sweat and tears dripping from my face. My sunglasses wouldn't stay on from the sweat, but I didn't want others to see I was a hot mess trying to run with tears and snot all on my face. I reached a point where it didn't matter if people saw me; I had to take them off and embrace my hot-mess face. I had my worship music playing the whole time, and it is amazing what that music can do to you. I listened to many different songs that were inspirational and gave hope and also some that just made me cry more.

This was the day that I completely tapped into Jesus and just gave it all to Him. I realized I could not do this alone; I could not process this grief, confusion, and frustration by myself. I continued to run and cry for about

four miles that day. It was the relief I needed. I needed
that time to question God, ask Him all the questions I
was thinking but never actually wanted to ask. Some of
the questions I really didn't want answers to, but I knew
I needed to be a big girl and be accepting of whatever He
had planned. He gave me a breakthrough that day. He
allowed me to feel His comfort and peace in the worst
time of my life. After that run, I was able to slowly start
putting myself back together and get ready to take on
this new journey of finding myself and allowing God to
show me. I was ready to be a die-hard Christian and follow Him. I wanted to be more like Him, and I wanted
Him to show me how to handle this situation and many
to come that would seem hard to process and handle.
You might not be a runner and think I am crazy to find
God while running my heart out. You can do whatever you feel is necessary to help you find Him in your
hard place. I just happen to love running and listening
to praise music, so that worked for me.

I mentioned earlier in the book that I only prayed
sometimes. I want to make it clear that I am not shun-
ning prayer or degrading it in any way. Prayer is literally the best way to communicate with God. You need
prayer as the foundation of your faith that will connect
you to God and allow you to make your requests and
listen to His responses. If we plan to make it through

this world before we go to heaven, then we need prayer to help us through it and keep us attached to heaven. It's the best and only way I know to connect with God and talk to Him down on earth. I heard someone say before that prayer is like facetiming God. That is your only connection to heaven; you have to pray to talk to loved ones up there, and you have to pray to talk to God. I am not saying you have to feel weird by sitting on the side of your bed with your hands crossed and eyes closed. You can pray anytime, anywhere. You do not have to close your eyes for it to count, you don't have to have the perfect prayer, and you don't have to be in the dark. You just have to talk to Him like He is your friend. Nothing has to be scripted or perfect. Yes, God knows everything about you and His plan, but just like you like to talk to your parents about your plans or your friend about your day or what you want in the future, God wants to talk to you. He wants that closeness with you because—let's be honest—he deserves that. He created you and let His son die for all of your sins; the least you can do is talk to Him about your feelings, what you would like, or even what you expect in the future. I pray when falling asleep and sometimes never finish my prayer, but how great do you think it is for you to fall asleep talking to God? I'm sure He loves those days with us.

There is a really good story in the Bible I want to share. It's about the story of Hannah in 1 Samuel. Hannah was not able to have children. She was married to a man who had two wives, her and Peniannah. (It was totally normal back in the Bible days to have more than one wife. I know; weird…) So Peniannah could have children, and Hannah couldn't; her womb was closed. Hannah would get extra food from her husband since she didn't have children to feed. It was like a "I'm sorry you can't have kids; here's something to make you feel better" thing. Hannah decided to take time and completely consume herself in prayer and cried that she wanted a son very badly. A priest assumed she was drunk because she was so deep in prayer and wasn't acting right. She continued to pray her little heart out and let the priest know not to let her be forgotten. After talking with the priest—even with the sketchy comment toward her—she believed in God and walked away happy and no longer upset. Verses 19 and 20 immediately tell us she was able to bear a son and his name was Samuel:

> *"So in the course of time Hannah became pregnant and gave birth to a son. She named him Samuel, saying, 'Because I have asked the Lord for him'" (Samuel 1:20 [NIV]).*

The important message to get from that scripture is, she asked for a child when it was physically impossible to have kids. God took her prayers and answered them not by just giving her a son but by giving her Samuel, who was recognized as the judge of all Israel. How amazing is the power of prayer?

I want you to read this scripture and really think about the words:

"The end of all things is near, therefore be alert and of sober mind so that you may pray. Above all, love each other deeply, because love covers a multitude of sins. Offer hospitality to one another without grumbling" (1 Peter 4:7–9 [NIV]).

What do you think?

We need to be open-minded and have clear heads concerning what we need to pray about. How we need to take on the spiritual battles going on that we do not even realize. We need to love one another because love covers sin. Love. Covers. Sin. Think about that for a minute. Let's just have some examples: Your child said they hate you, your spouse commits adultery, or your parent is addicted to drugs. What do you do? The Bible allows options for divorce when adultery is present. That does not mean God is like, "Sure Divorce over adultery. No big deal; you have my blessing." He is saying, you will not technically sin if you're divorcing over an adulterous spouse. But He hates divorce. He expects us to be able to love like Christ and forgive. He wants us to give grace like He has done for us. He wants us to show mercy like He does. I think, in times of blame, we forget all the things we have done or how we have sinned against God so that, when someone does it to us, we expect God to be on our side. Christ died for us and for everyone else that has sinned against us. You are just as worthy to be saved as the person that hurt you. I am not saying it will be easy. It will be some of the hardest stuff you will ever go through, and you might think you are not capable. But God's love and Christ, who died for us, are worth more than holding that anger toward someone or something we cannot control. Healing takes times; it's ok to think it's taking you more time than others. Everyone heals differently; we have all been hurt in different ways and by different people. But if you knew what God could do in your life, time wouldn't be of the essence. Have patience and know that good things come to those who wait.

"Truly my soul finds rest in God; my salvation comes from him" (Psalms 62:1 [NIV]).

Don't try to speed up the process of healing or forgiveness. God does not work on our time; He has His own and will not let us tell Him what is better. He knows the greater plan, and He will give us the strength and peace to make it through. Allow your soul to find rest in God and trust His plan for your life. What do you have to lose?

CHAPTER TWELVE

Where Is Your Faith?

I have shared my faith journey with you. Now it's your turn to think about yours. Some people will tell you they have had a strong faith since childhood because they grew up in church and their parents taught them a lot about Christianity. Others might tell you it took them finding their faith on their own as adults. Or there is the other bunch. Those of us who grew up in faith, turned away for a little bit here and there, and then found ourselves back. Whatever way your story is, just know it's special and God has been there to help you through it. No matter the pain, guilt, or frustrations you have faced in your life, Jesus will always love you and forgive you. Even If you think you committed the worst sins, you are still forgiven by Him; you just have to repent.

If you had to explain to someone where your faith stood right now in Christ, would you be excited to share? Would you be hesitant? Do you feel like you know more than others? Or do you know hardly anything at all? Honestly, however you answer, it does not make you any less worthy than others. You and God have your own relationship, and it's your responsibility to seek that for yourself. Don't worry if someone else is more advanced than you or if you feel that you started late in life. You could be ninety before finding God, and He would love you just as much as the people who have been faithful Christians since they were children.

I want to reference a parable Jesus talks about regarding workers in the vineyard. He talks about a landowner who goes out at different times of the day to hire people to work for him. He goes about his day hiring people as early as nine in the morning and as late as five in the evening. The morning workers were upset because they started working in the early hours and were paid the same as the workers who only worked an hour (Matthew 20:1-16 [NIV]). What I took from this story is Jesus is telling us that even if you might be late, you are worthy of the same price as someone who might of started before you. Your faith can become stronger than someone who went to seminary or is a biblical scholar. You must put in the work to get to a place that you feel comfortable with God.

We are not perfect people in this world, and we will be skeptical. There are plenty of other corrupted things around that will persuade our thoughts and actions and make us think about what "might" be better than following God. See, everything in this world is only good until the world is over or until you go to either heaven or Hell. The material things in the world do not go to heaven with you; they stay here and do not benefit you in eternity. We may think this life is long, but in reality, there's just a short blip between Christ ascending and Christ returning.

A quick definition of faith is basically completely putting your whole trust in something—in this instance, God. Don't panic thinking you can never question God or have days when you will be completely confused about Him. We all do it, and we all get a little frustrated when we do not understand what His plan is. That's totally normal, and honestly if we are questioning Him, that means we believe in Him and are talking to Him like we should. God loves having conversations with us, even if those conversations are hard. He has an endless amount of mercy, so He can handle your confused and frustrated emotions. I know it's hard to process that this unseen God is so great and understanding, but think about someone who is not a Christian. I wonder how hard it is to process all the things we talk about with God and how hard it is to understand unconditional love. Those people need us. They need us to help guide them to Jesus and show them the unconditional love Christ shows us.

Some of the most memorable people in the Bible questioned God all the time. But they stood strong in showing their faith in Him. That's what is important—standing strong in your faith. You may be saying that you need more proof from Him or more of an explanation, but do not be blind when He comes out and shows you. Do not turn away when He gives you what you ask for, just because it wasn't the way you pictured it. God is sneaky sometimes, and He will pop out of nowhere and be like, "You asked. Here is your proof." And the first thing we like to say is, "Oh, was that in my head? Or was that actually God?" I have done that so many times—I've tried to figure out if God told me that or if He was actually showing me the sign I'd asked for.

I asked Him one day to give me a very direct sign because I was so caught up in my head that I could not differentiate the difference between His word and mine. I prayed about it over and over, and—I'll tell you what— He answered in the most powerful way and made me know that it was Him telling me and showing me what I was asking for. I mean, it was like, "Here is your neon sign spelling out exactly what you asked for!" It was so moving to me, and it made me realize how real He is and how much He is looking out for me. Friends, I want you to experience that. I want you to be able to sit there one day and have God give you exactly what you asked of Him. But I can't be the one to change your heart and show you Him. I can only give you some of the tools to make your steps closer to Him. You need to put in the work; I need you to get down on those knees and pray. You have to surrender your life to Jesus and give Him all your faith. You can do it, even if you have before and don't want to again because of disappointment. He is listening, and He will act when the plans are for the good of your life and for His glory.

Let's jump back into the Bible really quickly. There are many books and stories in there that give examples of people who doubted God. I want to touch base on Thomas, a disciple that doubted Jesus's resurrection. (He literally was a disciple that saw Jesus work wonders and was like, "Nah, it's not Him. He can't raise Himself from the dead." Well, you're wrong, Thomas.)

"Now Thomas, one of the twelve, was not with the disciples when Jesus came. So the other

disciples told him, 'We have seen the Lord!'
But he said to them, 'Unless I see the nail
marks in his hands and put my finger where
the nails were, and put my hand into his side,
I will not believe'" (John 20:24–25 [NIV]).

A week later, Jesus came back to visit the disciples, and Thomas was there. Jesus came up and showed His hands and side. Of course, now Thomas believed it was Him and got all excited that the messiah was back and had risen from the dead. Let's skip a verse or two.

"Then Jesus told him, 'Because you have seen me,
you have believed. Blessed are those who have not
seen and yet have believed'" (John 20:29 [NIV]).

I'm not saying we are better than Thomas in the Bible, but I am saying we should think about how strong our faith is; we have never seen Jesus in the flesh, and yet we believe. We believe that one day He will come back and take us into eternity with God. We have the Bible that tells us this, and it's a living word that we can trust. Thomas and the disciples didn't have the Bible; they got to see Jesus in His own element, but just like all of us, they still doubted. They were present when He healed blind people, when He healed a woman possessed by demons, when He brought people back to life in front of them. You don't have to beat yourself up if you are unsure about God; a lot of people question Him. What you do need to realize is that this is your faith, and your decisions will affect your eternity. No one can come between you and God.

People will have their opinions, but that's all they are. They do not define your relationship with God. I know, we like to include people's opinions in our relationship with God. But guess what? Their opinions literally will not matter when you and God sit on judgment day going through the book of life. You really think they are going to be thinking about you when God starts questioning them? I sure as heck will not be worried about them; I will be more intrigued by the fact that I am at the gates of heaven seeing Jesus for the first time.

I think the most important thing out of all this is to remember who you are, what you're capable of, and that God is here to guide you and help you through any situation. He is not your enemy; He is not "out to get you"; He is not making things happen to you because you have bad luck. He loves us so unconditionally that He gave up His son to save us. I just want to make sure you hear me out: you are not weird for being a Christian, you are not weird for having other opinions about situations because you believe in Jesus, you are not strange because you have feelings about certain situations because Jesus has brought you through it, and you are not the only one searching for more answers about Jesus and wanting to talk about Him. We have to be there for one another. This world is cruel, and it's only going to get worse before Jesus comes. We have to buckle down and be there for one another.

If I did not go through the things in my life—including the most recent events—I would not be where I am spiritually or mentally. I've learned so much in the last season of my life that has completely shaped me into the Christian I am today. I did so much research and continue to learn every day about Christianity and God.

I hope that you all do not have to go through something damaging like I did, just to get the healing you need to change your perspective in your faith. I want you to learn from what I have gone through and try to change your destiny and make God's plan for your life easier. If I can help one person who reads this book to grow closer to God or dig deeper into their faith, then I have done what God has called me to do. God says that we need to be disciples of Christ, and the way to do that is sharing His word, showing His grace, and giving mercy to others. It will not be easy; don't get me wrong.

The Bible says that we will experience hardship and experience things that are unsettling, but know that He has overcome the world and has already given us what we need to succeed.

> *"I have told you these things, so that in me you may have peace. In this world you will have trouble. But take heart! I have overcome the world" (John 16:33 [NIV]).*

I think we get so wrapped up in our tribulations that we forget God has already overcome the world, just for us. There is nothing we can do, nothing we can change, that God has not already overcome for us. Some people find it hard surrendering their hearts over to God during the hard times; I did too. But I only have positive stories to tell about how I let God take over and was able to sit back and let Him carry my burdens. That's why He is here—to fight for us. It's simple. All you have to say is "Lord, help me!"

My prayer for you is that you will take this moment to think about your current situation. I want you to take this time to give it all to God, take whatever you are thinking, and let it go. Think of how much peace you can have if God takes over. I pray that you will experience the peace and mercy He gives us. I hope you experience His love and compassion and do not push it away. My hope is that you get your Bible, spend time with Him, and focus on His creations. Read the scriptures and stories. Learn about His history and about how His people have overcome bigger obstacles than we can imagine. I pray that you realize and consider the love Jesus has for us and that you are thankful to God because He allowed His son to be the final sacrifice for us so that we could live our lives knowing that God is for us and not against us. I pray you do not let Satan take your happiness away, do not allow him to make you think you are unworthy or anything less than what God has made you to be. Finally, I pray that this book has motivated you, moved you, or spoken to your heart as much as it has to mine as I wrote it. You are a beautiful child of God, and there is nothing that you could do that would keep Him from loving you.

Much Love,

Charity

ACKNOWLEDGMENTS

I have expressed how many great things God has done in my life and how thankful I am for being able to express my excitement. I was able to voice my faith to you all regarding the great things Jesus has done for me. I am so thankful for the people that God placed in my life to help show me Jesus, support me, and shape me into the woman I am today. I could have a very long list of people to thank but I want to thank the closest and most important people in my life that have made this book possible.

First, **Tyler,** you have been such a big influence in my life and have shown me how to grow and accomplish anything I want. You have given me so much love and compassion, even when I did not deserve it. I have been able to witness all the big accomplishments in your life, and you have coached me through most of mine. Thank you for being my friend, soulmate, and partner in this world. I would not be where I am today, without you pushing me to be better. Thank you for letting me spend countless nights writing, going crazy about it, and making you read and edit it for me. Your feedback has helped my book become more than I ever thought was possible.

To my **parents**: I know you're "doing your job" as my mom and dad, but I don't know how I will ever repay y'all for the love and support y'all have given me through the years. Thank you for setting my foundation on faith when I was a child and continuing to always encourage me, even while I'm an adult. You two are the best grandparents for my kids, and I love that they get to learn from y'all just as I was able to. Y'all have helped me learn how to parent and have pushed me when needed. Thank you for being the best parents Celeste and I could have.

Next, **Momo and Popo** are the real MVPs when it comes to prayer. You two know how to keep Jesus at the center of your lives and have shown me how to truly be a Christian. I can't thank y'all enough for all of your prayers for me through all the tough times in my life. I can always count on godly advice from you, and I know you both always support me. If there was a day I felt that I needed Jesus, I could always count on you both to show me Him.

They don't know it yet, but my children are such a blessing to me. I wouldn't be where I am if I didn't have those two littles to raise. **Zoey**, you have shown me so much so far in your short life, and I will forever be grateful that I got to grow up together with you. You sure know how to keep Tyler and me on our toes. **Owen**, your life is such a blessing to us, and seeing how you are a mini version of your dad, with your love and happiness, makes me so happy. Both of you have love so unconditional, and it makes Tyler and me the happiest parents to be a part of both of your lives.

My friend, **Jessica,** thank you for letting me talk to you about my problems as I was trying to establish this Christianity thing and continuing to grow in it. Thanks for accepting my random texts whenever I learned something new in the Bible. I also appreciate all that you did when I needed help editing my book. Your skills are astonishing, and I am so grateful. I can always count on your support with my blog and book.

Lastly, **Celeste,** I could literally go on and on about how much you have been a huge influence in my life. I wouldn't be in my place today if it weren't for you. You used to pick on me when we were kids, and now you're talking me through some of the hardest things in life. I wouldn't have survived the last season of hardship I went through, if you hadn't been within walking distance and a phone call away. Thanks for letting me call you in the middle of the night and for always being willing to talk. You are my person to go to about anything that I need help with. I can always count on you to give me godly answers and to show me how to think like Christ. I probably wouldn't be writing this book today if it weren't for your help and advice through my journey finding God again. Thanks for keeping me calm during the writing process and allowing me to talk your ear off about the book. You're my only sibling, and I am happy there isn't another sibling I have to share you with. Thanks for being Celeste the BEST who I know I can always count on.

Charity Dockery is a Licensed Vocational Nurse (LVN) with a degree in science. After starting her blog, www.charityfaithlove.com, she felt a need to share her story with a wider audience and show how great God really is. She believes He put this book in her heart as a reason to start writing, and it has flourished ever since.

Charity grew up in La Grange, Texas, and currently resides there with her husband and children. Her favorite hobbies are writing for her blog, enjoying time outside with family, and watching movies.